CHIEF TRUTHS
OF THE FAITH

A Course in Religion
Book I

About This Se...

Fr. John Laux, M.A. was a high school religion teacher who distilled the fruit of his many years of research and teaching into these fine high school religion books. At first glance, it might appear foolish to reprint books that were first published in 1928. But a reading of Fr. Laux's books will lay that thought to rest. For he had a rare talent of capsulizing the intricacies of our Catholic Faith and its theology into succinct, precise, learned and yet lively prose that is at once truly interesting and that all can easily understand. He is profoundly intellectual, yet always clear and easy. His writing, while aimed at the high school student, remains challenging and informative to the college student and the adult Catholic as well. But further, Fr. Laux writes in a virtually undated and almost un-dateable style, a style that is, one might say, classic and timeless, a style that truly befits his subject matter—the timeless teachings of our Ancient Church. For these reasons, the four books in this high school series are all works of rare genius, as also are his *Introduction to the Bible* and *Church History,* for they all possess these same qualities that make Fr. Laux such a pleasure to read and such a joy to study from.

THE SAVIOR OF THE WORLD

CHIEF TRUTHS OF THE FAITH

CREATION, ORIGINAL SIN, CHRIST, FAITH,
GRACE, ETERNAL LIFE, ETC.

A Course in Religion
For Catholic High Schools and Academies

BOOK I

by

Fr. John Laux, M.A.

Late Instructor of Religion, Notre Dame High School, and Professor of
Psychology, Villa Madonna College, Covington, Ky.

> "For I give you to understand, brethren, that
> the gospel which was preached by me is not
> according to man. For neither did I receive it
> of man, nor did I learn it; but by the revela-
> tion of Jesus Christ." —Galatians 1:11-12

TAN BOOKS AND PUBLISHERS, INC.
Rockford, Illinois 61105

NIHIL OBSTAT :   J. M. Lelen
                   Censor Librorum

IMPRIMATUR: ✠ Francis W. Howard
                   Bishop of Covington, Kentucky
                   March 25, 1932

Library of Congress Catalog Card No.: 90-70439

ISBN: 0-89555-391-0

Cover illustration: Christ appears to the Apostles in the Upper Room, and St. Thomas declares his faith by saying, "My Lord and my God!"

Printed and bound in the United States of America.

TAN BOOKS AND PUBLISHERS, INC.
P.O. Box 424
Rockford, Illinois 61105

1990

A Word to the Teacher

The need of some systematic presentation of the truths of our Holy Religion to boys and girls of our American Catholic High Schools has been felt by Catholic educators for a long time. The manuals now in use have been found to be either too technical or too simple, and the problem has been to prepare a text that would suit the needs of the growing mind, and, while enlisting the interest of the pupils in acquiring a knowledge of religious truths, would at the same time encourage the practice of virtue and cultivate a love for the Church.

The present *Course in Religion for Catholic High Schools and Academies* is an attempt to solve this problem. The general arrangement of the course is based, as far as possible, on the division and order of the larger Baltimore Catechism. The catechetical form of presentation has been abandoned, because, in the opinion of prominent educators, "it is conducive to memory work rather than to reasoning, encourages inefficient teaching, and makes almost no appeal to the interest of the pupil."

For practical purposes the work has been divided into Four Parts, each of which is bound and paged separately and provided with copious helps for study and review, a table of contents and an index.

The First Part embraces the mystery of the Trinity, the work of Creation, Redemption, Sanctification, and Consummation. It is introduced by a brief treatment of the nature, necessity, sources, and qualities of Faith. The Second Part treats of the Means of Grace: the Sacraments, the Sacrifice of the Mass, Indulgences and Sacramentals. Part Three is devoted to General and Special Christian Moral; Part Four to Apologetics.

The writer suggests that every pupil be provided with a copy of the New Testament, to be used throughout the course; a Student's edition of the Missal, to be used in connection with Part Two; and the *Imitation of Christ* as supplementary material for Part Three. It is presupposed that there is a well-stocked Religious Book Shelf in every High School Library.

The concluding words of Father Drinkwater's preface to his excellent little book of religious instruction *Twelve and After* are applicable to every textbook in Religion: "Let us remind ourselves that religion is not a book-and-writing matter. Such instruction as this book contains is very useful and in some ways necessary; but there are things even more necessary, such as plenty of singing, corporate prayer, both liturgical and unliturgical, and opportunities for personal service, not to speak of the more individual and interior practice of religion. If these more essential things are well managed, then the intellectual instruction will have all the more meaning and fruit. It should become the raw material of Catholic ideals. We can but build up our altar stone by stone and arrange our wood upon it as carefully as may be, and then pray for the fire of the Lord to fall in acceptance of the offering."

A word to the teacher of religion. The purpose of the teaching of religion must be the same in all our schools from the grades to the university—to form *religious characters,* to train men and women who will be ready to profess their Faith with firm conviction and to practice it in their daily lives in union with the Church.

This obvious purpose of all religious teaching imposes a twofold duty on the teacher of religion in the High School: to give his pupils a *fuller* and *more profound grasp of Christian Doctrine,* and to lead them on to the *intelligent use* of the helps that have been given us to lead Christian lives.

It is idle to dispute, as is sometimes done, whether the training of the intellect is more important than the training of the heart and the will; the imparting of religious knowledge, than the formation of religious habits. Both are of supreme importance. The will follows the intellect; but the intellect is also powerfully influenced by the will. Ignorance may sometimes be bliss, but never in religious matters. Well-instructed Catholics may become backsliders, but their number is small in comparison with those who are lost to the Church because their ignorance of Catholic teaching made them easy victims of the purveyors of false science, shallow philosophy, and neo-pagan morality. Religion requires that the *whole* man worship God with all his faculties and acts. The intellect must *believe* that which is true concerning God—

Faith; and the *will* must be directed to *do* those actions which are right and to avoid those which are wrong—*Morals.*

Cardinal Newman wished to see the enlightened Catholic youth pious, and the pious Catholic youth enlightened. This ideal may never be fully attained, but it is certainly worth striving after.

Catholic Action is today becoming a vital force throughout the world. The layman cannot effectively engage in Catholic Action unless he is well versed in the teachings of his faith and able at all times to explain and defend it. The type of layman, therefore, that is needed today is the type which Cardinal Newman asked for years ago when he said: "I want laymen, not arrogant, not rash in speech, not disputatious, but men who know their religion, who enter into it, who know just where they stand, who know what they hold and what they do not; who know their Creed so well that they can give an account of it; who know so much of history that they can defend it. I want an intelligent, well instructed laity. I wish you to enlarge your knowledge, to cultivate your reason, to get an insight into the relation of truth to truth; to learn to view things as they are; to understand how faith and reason stand to each other; what are the bases and principles of Catholicism. Ignorance is the root of bitterness."

The great Cardinal's ideal of the Catholic layman may never be fully attained, but it is certainly worth striving after. It is only through such pious and enlightened laymen and laywomen, working with their bishops and pastors, that Catholic Action can be truly successful. It is the chief duty of our Catholic Educational system to place on the battlefield an army of laymen, equipped to "fight the battles of the Lord."

THE AUTHOR.

The author and the publishers make grateful acknowledgment to the B. Herder Book Co. for permission to include material from "Stock Charges Against the Bible," by T. Paffrath, adapted by C. Kean.

CONTENTS

CONTENTS

"My God and My All"

St. Francis of Assisi in the Embrace of the Crucified Lord

INTRODUCTION

Our Life's Purpose

"Thou hast made us for Thyself, O God, and our heart is restless until it rests in Thee."—ST. AUGUSTINE.

1. The Desire for Happiness.—All men have at least one aspiration in common—they all wish to be perfectly happy. This desire is so deeply rooted in our hearts that it can never be destroyed. It is a part of our very nature, and must, therefore, have been planted therein by God Himself, the Author of our nature. Now, if the all-wise God created us with such an ardent longing for perfect happiness, He also wishes us to attain it.

2. Earthly Goods and Happiness.—Many seek happiness in the possession of earthly goods, such as riches, honors, pleasures. But these things cannot make us perfectly happy. They are all vain and perishable, often embitter our life, and invariably forsake us in death. Solomon, one of the most fortunate of kings, was bound to confess: "I heaped together for myself silver and gold, and the wealth of kings and provinces . . . ; and whatsoever my eyes desired, I refused them not; and I withheld not my heart from enjoying every pleasure. . . . *And I saw in all things vanity, and vexation of mind, and that nothing was lasting under the sun*" (Eccles. 2,8-11).

3. "God Alone Sufficeth."—Only a good that is perfect in every way, that never changes, and never ends, can satisfy our desire for perfect happiness. There is only one such Supreme Good—*God*. Hence, we cannot find perfect happiness except in the possession of God. "Thou hast made us for Thyself, O God, and our heart is restless until it rests in Thee," says St. Augustine. And the Venerable Thomas à Kempis begins his *Imitation of Christ* with the golden words: "Vanity of vanities, and all is vanity, besides loving God and serving Him alone."

4. How We Can Possess God.—We cannot possess God as we possess a house or a farm or a sum of money. These are material things, and God is a spirit. We can possess Him only as we possess something true, good, and beautiful, with our intellect and our will, by knowledge and love. Our eternal happiness will consist in contemplating and loving God, the Supreme Truth, Beauty, and Goodness. Hence, our happiness in this life, and the only means of attaining eternal happiness in the next, consists in knowing and loving God with all the powers of our intellect and our will. "This is eternal life: That they may know Thee, the only true God, and Jesus Christ, whom Thou hast sent" (John 17,3). And the first and greatest commandment is this: "Thou shalt love the Lord, thy God, with thy whole heart, and with thy whole soul, and with thy whole mind" (Matt. 22,37).

5. Love and Service.—If we know and love God, we will also serve Him. Love and service go hand in hand. We serve a person if we do his will. God has made His will known to us in the commandments which He has given us. Hence, we serve God if we keep His commandments. Our Lord said to the rich young man: "If thou wilt enter into life, keep the commandments" (Matt. 19,17). And the Beloved Disciple says: "This is the charity [love] of God, that we keep His commandments" (1 John 5,3).

Our life's purpose, therefore, is to know, love, and serve God here on earth, in order that our desire for perfect happiness may be satisfied by the possession of God in Heaven.

6. Grace and Our Life's Purpose.—Of ourselves, by our own natural strength, we could never know God properly, love Him truly, and keep His commandments faithfully. For this we need a special help from God. "Without Me," says Our Lord, "you can do nothing" (John 15,5). We call this special help *grace,* because it is a favor, or *free gift* of God. By it He enlightens our mind and strengthens our will to know Him and to love Him. By it He performs the greatest marvel of His love: He makes us holy and pleasing in His sight, adopts us as His children, gives us the right to inherit the Kingdom of Heaven. These wonderful gifts can be obtained by all through the *means of grace,* the most important of which are Prayer and the Sacraments.

Since our whole Religion, our whole duty as creatures, consists in knowing, loving, and serving God with the help of divine grace, the *study of Religion* is the most important of all our studies. This study falls naturally into three parts:

Hunc habuit Petrum felix Germania Patrem.
Quem stupuere olim, curia, Templa scholæ.

ST. PETER CANISIUS

Doctor of the Church. Author of the first complete series
of Catholic Catechisms

1. Knowledge of God—the *Truths of our holy Faith.*
2. Love and Service of God—our *Duties to God, to Ourselves, and to our Neighbor.*
3. Grace and the Means of Grace—the *Sacraments, the Holy Mass.*

SUGGESTIONS FOR STUDY AND REVIEW

1. Prepare a short paper on the following theme: *Our Life's Purpose, and How We Can Attain It.* The following questions will serve as a plan for your composition. Answer them without writing them out.

   a) What do all men desire?

   b) Why cannot the things of earth make us perfectly happy? See the Epistle of St. James 4,15, and the Gospel of St. Luke 12,16.

   c) Why can God alone satisfy our desire for perfect happiness? See the *Imitation of Christ,* Book I, ch. 1, no. 4. Write out this passage.

   d) If God alone can satisfy our desire for perfect happiness, what must be the purpose of our life?

   e) Did God tell us how we can attain this purpose? Did He give us the means to attain it? See John 17,3; Matt. 22,34; 19,17.

   f) Why are our Religion lessons the most important of all our lessons?

2. This paper may either be read to the class or delivered from memory without slavish adherence to the manuscript, but with careful following out of the plan. Try to find appropriate examples from the Bible and Church history to illustrate the theme. You know the story of St. Philip Neri and the Young Lawyer. How was St. Francis Xavier converted? What great Saints taught catechism and wrote catechisms? (St. Peter Canisius and St. Robert Bellarmine.)

   Familiar is the story of Napoleon teaching the Catechism. For more than two years during his imprisonment on the Island of St. Helena, Napoleon Bonaparte taught the Catechism every day to the daughter of General Bertrand, his faithful companion in captivity. When the girl was old enough to make her first Communion, he procured a priest from France to continue the instructions and to prepare her for that great event.

CHIEF TRUTHS OF THE FAITH

A Course in Religion
Book I

CHAPTER I

Our Knowledge of God

"The fool said in his heart: There is no God."—Ps. 52,1.

1. How We Know God.—Our first duty is to know God. In Heaven we shall know Him face to face, but in this life He is hidden from our direct knowledge. We can, however, know something about Him by carefully noticing the things He has made, and still more by firmly believing what He has told us about Himself. In other words, we know God both by the *natural light of reason* and by the *supernatural light of faith*.

2. What Our Reason Tells Us About God.—Our reason tells us that there is one true God, the beginning and end of all things, our Creator and Lord; and that we must worship Him and do His will as it is written by Him in our hearts.

That there is an almighty God must be clear to every thinking person, for the fact is clearly proved by the whole visible world with its wise arrangement as well as by the voice of conscience.

a) No one can reasonably think that the world made itself; nor that the heavenly bodies could begin to move through space by their own power.

b) The wonderful arrangement and perfect order of the world lead us to infer that it was planned and carried out by a Being of supreme intelligence and skill.

c) All men who are in a normal state of mind know that they are bound in conscience to do certain acts and to avoid other acts, and feel that they are responsible for their conduct to a Supreme Judge who is the avenger of evil and the rewarder of good.

d) All the nations and races of men have always had an inner conviction of the existence of a Supreme Being. If there are any barbarous tribes that practice no religion, they can be such only as are degraded by vice below the normal condition of human beings.

The Scripture says: "The fool said in his heart: There is no God" (**Ps.** 52,1). Those who deny the existence of God are called *Atheists* (Greek *a-,*

I

not, and *theos*, God). Such people usually have reasoned themselves, or have been led by others, into a state of *doubt* in regard to the existence of God. Their state of mind arises either from pride, or from corruption of heart, or from a misguided education, or from all three. "He who denies the existence of God," says St. Augustine, "has some reason for wishing that God did not exist."

3. God Reveals Himself.—But God wished us to know much more about Himself—and about ourselves too—than our reason alone can tell us. From time to time, in His wisdom and goodness, He drew aside the veil that hides Him from us. He revealed Himself and His eternal decrees to us. He told us things about Himself which we could not otherwise know at all or not with certainty.

Revelation (Latin *re-*, back, and *velum*, a veil) means both the manifestation by God of His will and truths to man, and the body of truths thus manifested. It is called *supernatural* or *divine revelation*, as opposed to the natural revelation of Himself that God makes through the visible world.

4. We Know God's Revelations by Faith.—God did not reveal Himself directly to all men, or even to very many, but only to a few. These men were told by Him to make His revelations known to their fellow-men. Since God does not speak directly to each one of us, we have to take the word of those to whom He did speak for what He told them. In other words, we take God's revelations on *faith*. To take something on faith means to believe or hold as true what another tells us.

If we believe what a fellow-man tells us on his own authority or on the authority of another fellow-man, we have *human faith*. If we hold firmly and without doubting what someone tells us on God's authority, we have *divine faith*, for in that case we really believe God Himself.

5. God's Spokesmen and Their Credentials.—But how do we know when a human being tells us something on God's authority? We ask him to present his *credentials*, that is, we ask him to prove to us that he is really a messenger of God, and speaks in God's name; just as we ask anyone who claims to be the ambassador or representative of an earthly potentate to show us his credentials before we believe him.

Miracles and *Prophecies* are the only infallible credentials which God gives His spokesmen. If God puts His miraculous power at the disposal of a human being or permits him to look into the secrets of the future, we can say without hesitation or fear of error that such a person has been sent by God.

Miracles are extraordinary works which cannot be done by the powers of nature, but only through the omnipotence of God; for example, to raise a person from the dead.

Prophecy is a clear and definite foretelling of an event that can be known to God alone, because it depends either on the free will of God or on the free will of man. To foretell an eclipse of the sun or of the moon, is not a prophecy; but it is a prophecy to foretell the exact manner of one's own death at the hands of others.

6. Who Were God's Spokesmen?—The things which God wished us to know for our salvation He made known to us by the *Patriarchs* and *Prophets*, and above all by His Son *Jesus Christ* and the *Apostles*.

Jesus Christ claimed to be not only a messenger of God, but the true Son of God Himself. He proved His claim by the supreme holiness of His life, by numerous miracles and prophecies during His life on earth, and by the crowning miracle of His Resurrection. He guarantees for us the revelations made to the Patriarchs and Prophets, as well as those made by His own Apostles.

7. Revealed Mysteries.—Since, then, God Himself has spoken to us, all that He has told us about Himself and about our own origin and destiny must be absolutely true, for God can neither deceive nor be deceived; if He could, He would not be God. Hence, even when He tells us things which we cannot understand —*mysteries*—we none the less firmly believe them, because He has revealed them.

Mysteries are revealed truths that are above and beyond our reason though not contrary to it. There are many natural mysteries, such as the growth of trees and plants and the marvelous instinct of birds and animals, which we do not understand; is there any wonder that mysteries should be found among the revealed truths? The Trinity is a mystery, because we cannot understand how one God can subsist in three Persons; but it is in no way contrary to our reason: we do not believe that three gods are one God, nor that three persons are one person, which would be a contradiction.

SUGGESTIONS FOR STUDY AND REVIEW

1. What do we know about God by the light of reason?
2. What is the difference between human and divine faith?
3. What does the word "reveal" mean? Explain its origin.
4. Give five examples from the Old Testament illustrating the manner in which God revealed things to men.

5. How did Moses prove to the Pharao that he was sent by God?
6. How did Our Lord prove that He is the Son of God?
7. Is the following statement true or false: "A mystery is a revealed truth that is contrary to our reason"?
8. Copy the following texts: Heb. 1,1-2; Rom. 1,20; Acts 14,16; John 1,18. Use these texts to illustrate various points touched upon in this chapter: for example, Rom. 1,20 shows that we can know God by the light of reason.
9. *Reading:* Rev. Bertrand L. Conway, *The Question Box,* pp. 41-45, on Miracles.

THE ARAB'S PROOF OF THE EXISTENCE OF GOD

An Arab in the desert was once asked how he knew there is a God. "In the same way," he said, "as I know by the footprints on the sand that a man or an animal has passed this way."

ST. ANTONY'S BOOK

The thousands of men who visited St. Antony in the desert were astonished at his wisdom and good sense. Asked where he had acquired such solid wisdom, he replied, pointing with one hand to the heavens and with the other to the earth: "There is my book; I have no other: all should study it: in considering the works of God, they will be filled with admiration and love of Him who created all things."

LORD BYRON ON THE EXISTENCE OF GOD

"How, raising our eyes to heaven, or directing them to the earth, can we doubt of the existence of God?—or how, turning them to what is within us, can we doubt that there is something more noble and durable than the clay of which we are formed?"

CHAPTER II

The Church, the Guardian and Teacher
of Divine Revelation

"Behold, I am with you all days, even to the consummation
of the world."—MATT. 28,20.

God revealed many heavenly truths to us through the Patriarchs
and the Prophets, but especially through His Son Jesus Christ.
Who has preserved these revelations? Who teaches them to us?
For God surely made His revelations for all men of all time.

**1. How God's Revelations Were Preserved and Handed
Down.**—When Jesus ascended into heaven, He left His revelation
as a most precious heritage to His faithful followers, the Apostles.
His last words to them were: "All power is given to Me in Heaven
and on earth: going, therefore, teach ye all nations, baptizing them
in the name of the Father and of the Son and of the Holy Ghost,
teaching them to observe all things whatsoever I have commanded
you: and, behold, I am with you all days, even to the consummation of the world."

THE AMBASSADORS OF CHRIST

5

St. Peter and the other Apostles diligently carried out their Divine Master's command. On Pentecost Day they were filled with the power of the Holy Ghost. Then they went forth to all parts of the world and preached to Jews and pagans what Jesus had taught them. Many believed and became Christians, that is, members of the Church which Christ had founded.

THE DESCENT OF THE HOLY GHOST

"And suddenly there came a sound from heaven, as of a mighty wind coming, and it filled the whole house where they were sitting. And there appeared to them parted tongues as it were of fire and it sat upon every one of them: And they were all filled with the Holy Ghost." (Acts 2,2-4.)

When the Apostles died, they bequeathed the revelations of Christ to their successors: to the Pope, the successor of St. Peter as the visible head of the Church, and to the Bishops, the successors of the other Apostles. The Popes and the Bishops, who form the teaching body of the Church, guarded the teachings of the Apostles as most precious treasures and continued to spread the knowledge of them over the whole earth. In this way the truths which Christ taught have come down to us undiminished and uncorrupted, because Christ had pledged His divine word that His Church should never be led into error. "Behold, I am with you all days, even to the consummation of the world."

Now we can answer the questions asked above: Who has preserved the revelations of Christ? Who teaches them to us? The Catholic Church has guarded them faithfully, and teaches them infallibly to all men.

Hence, if you are asked: What must the Catholic believe? the answer is: *The Catholic must believe all that God has revealed and through His Church proposes to his belief.*

2. Faith a Divine Gift to Help Us to Believe God's Revelations.—God asks us to believe on His word many sublime truths which our weak intellect cannot understand. But in His infinite goodness He has made faith easy for us, if only we show good will. At our Baptism the Heavenly Gardener, the Holy Ghost, planted a heavenly seed in our souls—the *gift of faith*, the power to believe. As we grew up, the truths of faith were gradually made known to us by our parents, our teachers, and our pastors, and with the help of the Holy Ghost we readily believed them. Then the Holy Ghost came to us once more in the Sacrament of Confirmation to strengthen our faith. Thus, we see that not only the truths which we must believe, but also the power to believe, come from God. Without the grace of God we could not believe at all. *Faith is a gift of God, and an effect of His grace, which enlightens our understanding and moves our will to believe, without doubting, all those things which God has revealed, and proposes by His Church to our belief.*

SUGGESTIONS FOR STUDY AND REVIEW

1. Through whom did God reveal Himself to us?
2. To whom did Christ entrust His revelations?
3. How did the teachings of Christ come down to us?
4. What is the Church for us?

5. What must the Catholic believe?
6. Can we believe without help from God?
7. When did we receive the gift of faith?
8. Write down an Act of Faith.
9. Copy the following texts and apply them in answering the above questions: Matt. 28,18-20; John 6,66; Eph. 2,8; John 14,16; Heb. 11,1.
10. *Reading:* Stoddard, *Rebuilding a Lost Faith,* ch. VII, "Revelation."

CHAPTER III

The Sources of Faith: Holy Scripture

"The holy men of God spoke, inspired by the Holy Ghost."—2 Pet. 1,21.

How Does the Church Know All That God Has Revealed? Or, to put the question in another way: From what sources does the Church draw the truths which she teaches us as revealed by God?

The truths revealed by God are contained in *Holy Scripture* and in *Tradition*. From these two sources the Church draws the truths which she teaches. She cannot teach anything that is not contained in these two sources. We shall treat first of Holy Scripture.

A. Holy Scripture in General

1. Definition and Division

1. What Is Holy Scripture?—Holy Scripture is a collection of books written under the inspiration of God, and recognized as such by the Church.

This collection of books is called Holy Scripture or Holy Writ because it is holy in its origin, its purpose and its contents. It is also called the *Bible,* from the Greek word *biblia,* which is the plural of *biblion,* and means "books." In the Middle Ages the word *biblia* was used as a singular noun, and was so translated into English.

No book has been so widely diffused or has exercised such a far-reaching influence on the religion, morality and civilization of mankind as the Bible. It was copied and recopied innumerable times. It was the first book to appear in print—the Gutenberg Bible, 1450 A.D.—and before the end of the fifteenth century it was reprinted more than a hundred times. To-day it is spread over the whole world in about three hundred translations.

2. Old and New Testaments.—Of the seventy-two books which make up the Bible, forty-five were written before the time of Christ. They contain the revelations made by God to men before the coming of Christ, and are called the books of the Old Testament. The other twenty-seven books were written after the time of Christ. They contain the revelations which we have received

9

through Christ and His Apostles, and are called the books of the *New Testament.*

Testament, in this connection, does not mean a written document wherein a person provides for the disposal of his property after his death, but a *covenant,* or *compact.* The dealings of God with His chosen people are called in Scripture the "covenant or testament of God with men." The covenant was that Jehovah was to bring them into the Promised Land and to be their protector, and they, on their part, were to keep Jehovah's laws and have nothing to do with false gods.

2. Divine Origin of Holy Scripture: Inspiration

1. What Inspiration Means.—The books of the Bible are different from all other books. All other books are purely human books, the products of human intelligence alone. The books of the Bible were not composed by mere human effort, but the Holy Ghost took such an active part in their composition that He is their real Author. The human writers merely co-operated with the Holy Ghost. Hence *Holy Scripture is truly the Word of God.*

The mysterious working together of God and man in the production of the books of the Bible is called inspiration, from the Latin word *inspiratio,* a "breathing in."

When we say that Moses and the other sacred writers were inspired, we mean: (1) that it was God who moved the authors to write these books; (2) that while writing they were protected by God against all error; (3) that they wrote only what God wished them to write; and (4) that if God wished them to write something which they did not or could not know, He had to reveal it to them.

2. Extent of Inspiration.—This movement of God, this divine guidance and protection, this *inspiration extends to the whole of the Bible and to every part of it.* It extends to everything written down by the human author.

"It is absolutely wrong," says Pope Leo XIII, "and it is forbidden either to narrow inspiration to certain parts only of Scripture, or to admit that the sacred writer has erred. The system of those who limit inspiration to matters of faith and morals cannot be tolerated."

Inspiration does not prevent the sacred writers from expressing themselves on subjects of natural science according to the knowledge and popular views of the time in which they lived. The same cannot be said of *historical facts.* These must be either true or false. The historical reports of the Bible must present absolute truth.

3. God Did Not Dictate the Bible.—Inspiration does not mean that every word of the Bible was dictated by the Holy Ghost. Such *verbal inspiration* would make a mere scribe of the sacred writer. "In conveying His thoughts to us, God did no violence to the writers. Each retains his individual manner, his mode of diction, his peculiarities of thought and language, so that we do not find two of them alike. They wrote in the tongue which they had used from childhood, or which they had acquired by education; in the language of the country and people wherein they were born, or wherein they at the time dwelt, and to whom their writings were addressed."

What has been said about the inspiration and infallibility of the Bible refers only to the original text. If later on those who copied the original text made mistakes or changes, these would not be the work of the original writers and hence would not be inspired.

4. How We Know That the Bible Is Inspired.—The fact of inspiration is vouched for above all by the infallible authority of the Church. The General Councils of Florence (1442) and Trent (1545-1564) call God the Author of both Testaments, and in 1870 the Vatican Council declared that the books of the Bible, "having been written by the inspiration of the Holy Ghost, have God for their Author, and have been delivered as such to the Church herself."

"To the books of Scripture," says St. Augustine, "I have learned to pay such reverence and honor as most firmly to believe that none of their authors committed any error in writing. If in that literature I meet with anything which seems contrary to truth, I will have no doubt that it is only the manuscript which is faulty, or that the translator has not hit the sense, or that I have failed to understand it."

3. The Canon, or Official List, of the Sacred Books

The books of the Bible were written by different men at different times, from the time of Moses, about fourteen hundred years before Christ, to the death of the last Apostle, St. John, about the year one hundred after Christ.

1. The Church Collects and Preserves the Books of the Bible.—The books of the Old Testament were collected and preserved by the highest religious authorities of the Jews. Christ and His Apostles confirmed the universal belief of the Jews that these books were of divine origin. The Church added to the books of the Old Testament the four Gospels, the Acts of the Apostles, the Letters (Epistles) written by the Apostles to various Christian communities and private persons, and the revelations made by God to St. John. In this way the Bible was put together and preserved by the Church.

2. The Church Draws Up an Official List of the Sacred Books.—During the two centuries before Christ and the early centuries after Christ a number of books were composed which claimed to be divinely inspired. These so-called apocryphal books contained pious and harmless legends, supposed sayings and doings of Christ and of those who were connected with Him, such as the Blessed Virgin, St. Joseph, the Apostles and their disciples. They were held in high esteem by some of the early Fathers of the Church, but absolutely rejected by others. To settle the controversy the Church declared definitely what writings must be acknowledged by all as inspired books. The official list of the inspired books is called the *Canon* of the Bible, from the Greek word *kanon,* which means "rule" or "standard."

The first Canon of the Sacred Writings was drawn up by the Council of Hippo in 393. This was confirmed by the Council of Rome in 394 and by the Council of Trent in the sixteenth century. According to these official decrees of the Church, the Bible contains seventy-two books, of which forty-five belong to the Old Testament, and twenty-seven to the New Testament.

3. Division of the Bible according to Content.—Many of the books of the Bible relate facts and events, and for this reason are called *historical* books; others teach doctrine and give wholesome admonitions for leading a holy life, and are therefore called *doctrinal* (didactic) books; others again foretell future events and are on that account called *prophetical* books.

The terms *historical, doctrinal* and *prophetical* are used to express the more prominent features of the books thus classified. The historical books contain many important doctrines and are interspersed with prophecies, while the prophetical books contain no small amount of history, and some of the doctrinal books, especially the Psalms, partake of a prophetical character.

In the following list the books of the Bible are classified according to their contents:

OLD TESTAMENT

HISTORICAL BOOKS

Genesis	Ruth	1 Esdras
Exodus	1 Kings	2 Esdras
Leviticus	2 Kings	Tobias
Numbers	3 Kings	Judith
Deuteronomy	4 Kings	Esther
Josue	1 Chronicles	1 Machabees
Judges	2 Chronicles	2 Machabees

DOCTRINAL BOOKS

Job	Ecclesiastes
Psalms	Canticle of Canticles
Proverbs	Wisdom

Ecclesiasticus

PROPHETICAL BOOKS

Isaias	Joel	Habacuc
Jeremias	Amos	Sophonias
Baruch	Abdias	Aggeus
Ezechiel	Jonas	Zacharias
Daniel	Micheas	Malachias
Osee	Nahum	

NEW TESTAMENT

HISTORICAL BOOKS

Matthew
Mark
Luke
John
Acts

DOCTRINAL BOOKS

Romans	1 Thessalonians	James
1 Corinthians	2 Thessalonians	1 Peter
2 Corinthians	1 Timothy	2 Peter
Galatians	2 Timothy	1 John
Ephesians	Titus	2 John
Philippians	Philemon	3 John
Colossians	Hebrews	Jude

PROPHETICAL BOOK

Apocalypse

4. Catholic and Protestant Bibles.—Luther rejected several books of the Old Testament—*Tobias, Judith, Wisdom, Ecclesiasticus, Baruch,* the two books of *Machabees* and parts of *Daniel* and *Esther*—because they contained too many things that conflicted with his own false teachings; e.g., the words of 2 Mach. 12,46: "It is a holy and wholesome thought to pray for the dead, that they may be loosed from sins." All Protestant denominations followed the lead of Luther, and to this day these books are missing from the Protestant Bible, or at most are printed in an appendix. Luther also rejected *Hebrews, James, Jude* and the *Apocalypse* from the New Testament. He called the Epistle of St. James a "straw epistle," because it contradicted his teaching on justification by faith alone. Later on, however, these books were accepted by the Protestants. Hence a Protestant Bible contains the same number of New Testament books as the Catholic Bible.

4. The Languages of the Bible

1. Hebrew, Aramaic, Greek.—The books of the Bible were originally written in Hebrew, Greek, and Aramaic. Nearly all the books of the Old Testament were written in Hebrew. Tobias, Judith, the Gospel of St. Matthew and portions of the books of Daniel, Esther, and 1 Esdras were written in Aramaic. Wisdom, 2 Machabees, and all of the New Testament, excepting Matthew, were written in Greek.

Hebrew is a Semitic (from Sem, a son of Noe) language spoken by the original inhabitants of Chanaan and transmitted by them to Abraham and his descendants.

Aramaic is a branch of the Semitic, and was spoken in Babylonia, Mesopotamia, Syria and the neighboring countries. It is also called Syriac. The Jews learned Aramaic during their captivity in Babylon in the sixth century before Christ. Hebrew was gradually superseded by Aramaic in Palestine. Since the third century before Christ it was a dead language, used only in the Jewish liturgy. Our Blessed Lord spoke Aramaic during His earthly life. There are a few Aramaic words and expressions in the Gospels, e.g., *talitha qumi, kepha, ephetha.*

Biblical *Greek* is not the Greek taught in our high schools and colleges, but a Greek dialect spoken and written throughout the greater part of the civilized world from the end of the fourth century before Christ till the sixth century after Christ. It is also called the Hellenistic dialect. The Jews who used it were known as Hellenists.

No *autographs* (i.e., originals written by the hands of the inspired writers) of any of the books of Scripture have come down to us. This is due partly to the perishable material used by the authors, partly to the fact that the Roman emperors decreed the destruction of the Sacred Books of the Christians (Edicts of Decius, A.D. 250 and Diocletian, A.D. 303).

2. Manuscripts of the Bible.—We possess very ancient copies' of all the books of the Bible. These copies are called *Biblical Manuscripts* (handwritings). Such manuscripts, if written on parchment in capital letters and bound in book form are called *codices*. The oldest Hebrew manuscript of the Bible dates from the tenth century. The oldest Greek manuscript was written in the fourth century. It is preserved in the Vatican Library.

5. *The Most Important Translations of the Bible*

1. The Greek Septuagint and the Latin Vulgate.—The books of the Old Testament were translated into Greek long before the time of Christ, and those of the New Testament from the original Greek into Latin, Syriac and other languages no later than the second century after Christ. The two most important translations are the Greek *Septuagint* and the Latin *Vulgate*.

The Septuagint translation was made in the third century before Christ to meet the religious needs of the Greek-speaking Jews of Alexandria in Egypt. About the year 290 B.C. the five books of Moses were translated into Greek, as the legend has it, by seventy learned Jews from Jerusalem, whence the name *Septuagint,* that is, "the work of the Seventy" (Lat. *septuaginta*).

Through the Septuagint translation the Greek-speaking pagans obtained a knowledge of divine revelation and were thus prepared for the preaching of the Gospel. The Apostles made use of the Septuagint in their preaching and writing, thus consecrating it, as it were, for all time.

The *Vulgate* is the most famous Latin translation of the Bible. It is almost exclusively the work of St. Jerome, who undertook it at the request of Pope Damasus (366-384). The translation of St. Jerome became by degrees the only Latin version used in the Western Church, and for this reason it was known as the *Vulgate,* from the Latin word *vulgata,* which means "disseminated" or "in common use." The Council of Trent declared the Vulgate to be the authentic Latin version, and the one to be used in public in the Western Church.

2. The Douay Bible.—Our English translation of the Scriptures is known as the Douay Version, because it was prepared at the English College of Douay in France. The New Testament was published at Rheims in 1582, the Old Testament at Douay in 1609. Several revisions of the Douay Bible have appeared, the best being that of Bishop Challoner in 1750.

CODEX VATICANUS 4TH CENTURY
The oldest Greek Bible printed on parchment in three columnar style.

A HANDWRITTEN LATIN BIBLE
The Bible from which this page has been taken is preserved at a monastery in Fulda, Germany. It is said to have been used by St. Boniface, A.D. 755. The text is from St. Luke II, II.

TITLE PAGE OF THE SIXTINE
EDITION OF THE VULGATE (1590)

16

The English Protestant translation of the Bible most widely used is the so-called "Authorized Version" of 1611. It was dedicated to King James I, and is on that account known as the "King James Bible." A revised version was published in 1885.

6. Interpretation of Holy Scripture

1. The Bible Needs an Interpreter.—No one who has read even one book of the Bible will deny that Holy Scripture needs *interpretation*. The Scriptures are frequently so difficult that it is simply absurd to say that it is an easy thing for everybody to read and understand them. St. Peter himself says that in the Epistles of St. Paul "there are some things hard to understand, which the ignorant and unstable wrest to their own destruction," and he adds: "as they do also the other Scriptures" (2 Pet. 3,16). It is clear that St. Peter did not approve of haphazard and unguided reading of the Bible.

The Deacon Philip asked the Chamberlain from Ethiopia, who was reading a passage of the Prophet Isaias, "Thinkest thou that thou understandest what thou readest?" And the Chamberlain answered: "And how can I, unless some man show me?" (Acts 8,30-31). St. Augustine, the greatest Father of the Church, confesses: "There are more things in the Bible which I cannot understand, than those which I can understand."

2. The Church, the Infallible Interpreter.—Since Holy Scripture is the work of the Holy Ghost, its meaning can be rightly and infallibly explained by Him alone or under His guidance. Now, God did not promise the Holy Ghost to every reader of the Bible, but only to the Catholic Church. Hence, the Catholic Church alone can explain the Scriptures with infallible certainty. No one is allowed to put an interpretation on any passage in the Bible contrary to that of the Church.

"What else," says St. Augustine, "gives rise to so many heresies, except that the Scripture, which is excellent in itself, is falsely interpreted?" And Shakespeare reminds us that "the devil can quote Scripture to his purpose."

7. The Reading of the Bible

1. Reading of the Bible Not Necessary for Salvation.— Since it is the Church that teaches us what we must believe in order to be saved, it is not necessary for the Catholic to read the Scriptures to search out the truth for himself. We can gain a knowledge of the truths of revelation by listening attentively to the living teaching of the Church. "Faith cometh by hearing," says St. Paul, "and hearing is through the word of Christ" (Rom. 10,17). Hence there is no divine precept commanding the Christian to read the Bible.

2. Bible Reading Most Profitable.—Although there is no strict obligation to read the Scriptures, still such reading is, in the words of St. Paul, "profitable unto salvation." St. Gregory the Great calls the Scriptures "a letter which Almighty God addressed to mankind." Hence no book has been so often and so highly recommended to the faithful as the Bible.

Leo XIII granted an indulgence of 300 days to all the faithful who spend at least a quarter of an hour each day in devoutly reading the Gospels, and a plenary indulgence under the usual conditions once a month for the daily reading.

The Third Plenary Council of Baltimore (1884) says in its Pastoral Letter: "It can hardly be necessary to remind you, beloved brethren, that the most highly valued treasure of every family library, and the most frequently and lovingly to be made use of, should be the Holy Scriptures."

3. Reading Translations of the Bible.—We are not, however, allowed to read any and every *translation* of the Bible, but only such translations as have been approved by the ecclesiastical authorities. The approval of the ecclesiastical authorities is expressed, as a rule, by the Latin word *Imprimatur,* i.e., "It may be printed," placed either at the beginning or end of the book together with the name of the bishop and the place and date of the grant. Only the Pope may approve a translation of the Bible that is not provided with explanatory notes.

The often-repeated accusation that Catholics are forbidden to read the Bible is absolutely false. Occasionally Catholics were forbidden to read certain translations; but such enactments were always local. In no instance did the Catholic Church ever prohibit the reading of the Bible in the original texts or in an approved translation.

SUGGESTIONS FOR STUDY AND REVIEW

1. From what sources does the Church draw her teachings?
2. What is Holy Scripture? Explain the world "Bible."
3. How is the Bible divided? Explain the word "Testament."
4. In what are the books of the Bible different from all other books? What is meant by saying that God *inspired* the writers of the Scriptures?
5. How do we know that the Bible is inspired? Did Our Lord and His Apostles regard the Old Testament as inspired?

6. What is meant by the *Canon* of the Scriptures? Why and when was the Canon of the Scriptures established?

7. What three classes of books are contained in the Bible?

8. Why did Luther reject some of the books of the Bible? Which books did he reject?

9. What do the following abbreviations stand for: Gen. 1,12; Lev. 4,6; Is. 2,5; 1 Mach. 2,3; Matt. 19; Acts 2,8; 1 Cor. 9,10; Apoc. 7?

10. In what languages was the Bible written? Which books were written in Greek? What language did Our Lord use?

11. What is the *Septuagint*? The *Douay Version*? The *Vulgate*?

12. Before the invention of printing, how were copies of the Bible multiplied? What is a manuscript? A codex? Which is the oldest codex of the Bible?

13. Why does the Bible need an interpreter? Who alone can interpret it infallibly?

14. Are we obliged to read the Bible? Why should we read it?

15. Copy the following texts and use them to help you to answer some of the above questions: 2 Pet. 1,21; 2 Pet. 3,16; Rom. 10,17; Rom. 15,4; 2 Tim. 3,16f.; Acts 1,16; John 5,39.

16. Criticize the following statements:
"Everybody has the right and the duty to interpret the Bible according to his own private judgment."
"Catholics are forbidden to read translations of the Bible."

17. Read the second chapter of the fourth book of the *Imitation of Christ*. What does it tell you about the purpose for which God gave us the Scriptures?

18. *Reading:* Cardinal Gibbons, *Faith of Our Fathers,* ch. VIII, "The Church and the Bible."

CHAPTER IV

Sources of Faith: Holy Scripture—(Continued)

B. The Books of the Old Testament

1. The Historical Books of the Old Testament

The Five Books of Moses.—The first five books of the Old Testament are called the Books of Moses, because the great Jewish prophet and law-giver is their author. These books are also called collectively the *Pentateuch,* a Greek word which means "the book of five volumes." The Pentateuch relates the history of Divine Revelation from the creation of the world and of man till the conquest of Palestine by the Israelites.

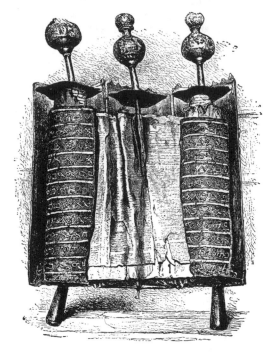

SAMARITAN PENTATEUCH ROLL

Genesis (Greek for "origin," i.e., of the world and of revelation) records the creation of the world and of our first parents, and the origin of sin; the history of mankind to the time of Noe; the Deluge; the tower of Babel; the confusion of languages, and the division of the human race.—The author then turns to the descendants of Sem, the oldest son of Noe, and deals with the greatest of these, *Abraham,* the Father of the Chosen People.— Then follows the history of Abraham's son Isaac, of Esau's forfeiture of his birthright, and the succession of Jacob.—Jacob's fortunes are next related in detail.—Lastly, the personal history of Joseph is told, and the migration of his father Jacob (also called Israel, the "Striver with God") and his brethren into the land of Egypt.

THE DEPARTURE OF THE HEBREWS FROM EGYPT

Exodus (Greek for "going out") relates the oppression of the Israelites in Egypt; the birth and education of Moses and his flight into the land of Madian; the appearance of God to Moses at Mount Horeb; revelation of the sacred name of Jehovah (Jahve), and the commissioning of Moses and Aaron to deliver the Israelites from bondage; the return of Moses to Egypt, and

his vain appeal to the Pharao to let the Children of Israel go free;
the first nine plagues; the institution of the Pasch, the last plague
(the destruction of the first-born of the Egyptians), and Israel's
departure from Egypt; the crossing of the Red Sea, the discom-
fiture of the Egyptians, the Song of Triumph, the Manna, and
other incidents of the journey through the Wilderness; the sojourn
at Mount Sinai and the giving of the Law, including the Ten
Commandments (Decalogue) and the Book of the Covenant;
directions for the building of the Tabernacle and the consecration
of Aaron and the priests; the falling away of the people from
Jehovah and the worshiping of the Golden Calf; the prayer of
Moses for the people and their return to God's favor; the
construction of the Tabernacle and its furniture.

Leviticus, the "Levitical Book," as its name implies, lays down
the laws for the religious worship, its ministers and seasons. The
historical portions interspersed through the book narrate the
consecration of Aaron and his sons, the punishment of Nadab
and Abiu, and the death of the blasphemer.

Numbers is so called because it begins and ends with the
numbering (census) of the Israelites. It contains the history of
the Israelites in the Desert for almost thirty-nine years. The
events related are amongst the most familiar to all Christians, old
and young. It is a sad story, "full of murmurings and revolts
against God and His Prophet and of punishments meted out
to the rebels; but also a consoling story, telling of God's mercy
to His people."

Deuteronomy (Greek for "second law") does not really
contain a second law, but is rather an explanation of the former
laws. It relates the incidents of the last year of Israel's wanderings
in the Wilderness. An historical supplement contains the magnifi-
cent Song of Moses, the Blessing of Moses, the account of his
death and burial, and the succession of Josue (chs. 32-34).

The Book of Josue.—The sixth book of the Old Testament
takes its name from Josue, the son of Nun, who on the death of
Moses assumed the leadership to which he had been designated by
his chief, and proceeded to the invasion and conquest of Chanaan,
the "Promised Land."

The book of Josue falls naturally into two parts: The crossing of the
Jordan, the capture of the powerful city of Jericho, and the conquest of the

greater part of Palestine; division of the lands west of the Jordan amongst the tribes of Israel, the setting aside of certain cities as "places of refuge" and of others as the homes of the priests, the solemn covenant whereby the people promise to cleave to the Lord alone. An epilogue records the death and burial of Josue on Mount Ephraim; the burial of the bones of Joseph in the field of Jacob in Sichem, and the death and burial of Eleazar, the son of Aaron.—Josue and Jesus are the same name in Hebrew and mean "Savior." Josue is a type of Our Saviour, who leads us to the heavenly "Land of Promise."

The Book of Judges.—After Josue's death the Israelites lived for several hundred years according to the constitution given them by God; but they were without regular rulers, and there was no central authority. Social, political, and religious confusion was the result. The people inclined to idolatry. This led them to neglect the duty imposed upon them of conquering the whole of Palestine, and they began to fraternize with the pagan inhabitants. God promptly punished them for their infidelity by delivering them into the hands of their enemies. However, as soon as they showed signs of repentance, He raised up amongst them valiant leaders, called *Judges,* who freed them from oppression and renewed the covenant with God. The *Book of Judges* contains the history of these military leaders, especially Barac (and Debbora), Gedeon, Jephte, and Samson.—*Judges* contains one of the few fables found in the Bible—the fable of the trees that wished to choose a king (9,8ff.).

The Book of Ruth relates an edifying family history of the period of the Judges. In a time of famine Elimelech leaves Bethlehem with his wife Noemi and his two sons to settle in the land of Moab. There the sons marry Moabite women, but die without children. After the death of her husband and her sons, Noemi prepares to return to Bethlehem. *Ruth,* one of her daughters-in-law, is determined to share her fortunes, rather than stay in Moab in comparative plenty. Her constancy and filial piety are rewarded. In Bethlehem she is married to Booz, a wealthy relative of her father-in-law, and through this union she becomes an ancestress of David and of Our Lord.—The story of Ruth is simply and charmingly told. The unknown writer was evidently an artist who took delight in the touching and graceful details of his picture. He succeeded in producing one of the most beautiful books of the Bible.

RUTH AND NOEMI
"Thy people shall be my people, and thy God, my God." (Ruth 1,16.)

The Four Books of Kings (known also as 1 and 2 of Samuel, and 1 and 2 of Kings) relate the history of Israel from the two last judges, Heli and Samuel, till the Babylonian Captivity. The contents may be summed up as follows:

1 The History of Heli and Samuel.
2. The foundation of the Kingdom; the story of Saul; his reign and rejection, and the rise of David.
3. History of David; the growth of his power, and its zenith.
4. Decline of David's power; his sin and repentance. His Psalm of Thanksgiving (First and Second Books of Kings).
5. The last years of David and the enthronement of Solomon.
6. The glorious reign of Solomon: his wisdom; the building of the Temple; the visit of the Queen of Sheba.
7. Solomon's fall and death.
8. Division of the Kingdom under Solomon's son Roboam, and the history of the two kingdoms of Juda and Israel till the fall of Samaria and the extinction of the Kingdom of Israel.
9. History of the Kingdom of Juda till the Babylonian Captivity in 587 B.C.

The Two Books of Chronicles (or Paralipomenon, i.e., "things left out" in the books of Kings) give a synopsis of the *religious* history of Juda. After a genealogical introduction covering the long period from Adam to Saul, the history of David is reviewed, then that of Solomon and of the other kings of David's line till the year 538 B.C.

The Two Books of Esdras.—The books of Kings and Chronicles leave the Holy City and the Temple a heap of ruins, and the people of Juda exiles and captives in Babylon. At last, after seventy years of captivity, the day of deliverance dawned. Cyrus, the Persian conqueror of Babylon, issued an edict (538 B.C.) permitting the Jews to return to Jerusalem. A remnant of the original exiles immediately set out under the leadership of Zorobabel. What happened after that till the rebuilding of the Temple and the walls of Jerusalem is told in the books of Esdras, or, as they are called, the books of Esdras and Nehemias, the authors of the books.

The Book of Tobias.—Tobias, of the tribe of Nephtali, is carried off with his wife and son to Ninive during the Assyrian invasion of Palestine. He is distinguished among his fellow-exiles for his fidelity to the Law and his works of mercy. Like Job, he is tried by tribulation—he loses his fortune and his eyesight— and like him he is rewarded in the end.

Tobias asks his son, who was also called Tobias, to go to Rages in Media to collect a considerable sum of money which, in the days of his prosperity, he had lent to a certain Gabelus. The Archangel Raphael, sent by God to accompany the young Tobias, helped him to win the hand of Sara, Raguel's daughter, and to obtain the money from Gabelus.

The purpose of the narrative is evidently to show with what loving solicitude God watches over those who serve Him faithfully. Nowhere in the Old Testament is the sanctity of marriage so earnestly stressed as in the words of the young Tobias to his bride: "We are children of Saints, and we must not be joined together like heathens that know not God" (8,5).

Judith.—Nabuchodonosor, king of Babylon, having conquered the Medes, sends his best general, Holofernes, to subdue the nations of the West who had refused to acknowledge his over-lordship. The Jews resist Holofernes, and he lays siege to Bethulia, a city of the Samaritan hill country. Reduced to the last extremity, the besieged are contemplating surrender. The pious and heroic widow *Judith* protests against this decision and prepares to repel the invader. She enters the tent of Holofernes, takes part in a banquet given in her honor, and in the night cuts off the head of the drunken general. During the confusion which ensues, the Jews sally forth and put the Assyrian army to rout. In glowing words, which the Church applies to the Blessed Virgin, the High Priest extols her patriotic deed: "Thou art the glory of Jerusalem, thou art the joy of Israel, thou art the honor of our people" (15,10).

Esther.—The scene of Esther is laid in the Persian court of Assuerus (Xerxes I, 485-465 B.C.). Vasthi, the queen of Assuerus, refuses to be present at a royal banquet, and is deposed. Esther, the niece of Mardochai, a wealthy and influential Jew of the tribe of Benjamin, is chosen to fill her place. She is thus enabled to save her countrymen in Persia from the wholesale destruction planned against them by their implacable enemy Aman, the royal favorite and grand-vizier. Aman is hanged on the gibbet which he had prepared for Mardochai, and the Jews revenge themselves on their enemies. The Feast of *Purim* (mentioned in 2 Mach. 15,37) is established by Esther and Mardochai to commemorate the deliverance of their people.

ESTHER DENOUNCES AMAN

"And Esther said: It is this Aman that is our adversary and most wicked enemy." (Esther 7,6.)

The Two Books of Machabees.—The Old Testament closes with two historical books of great interest: the *Books of the Machabees*. They give an account of the cruel persecution suffered by the people of God under the Syrian kings, to whom they had been subject since 198 B.C., and their glorious fight for religious and political freedom under the leadership of the priest Mathathias and his sons, especially Judas, surnamed Machabeus (i.e., the Hammer). The Books of the Machabees embrace the period of Jewish history from 175 to 135 B.C.

For four years (166-162 B.C.) Judas Machabeus fought for the independence of his nation. The account of his exploits forms a most stirring chapter in Jewish history. In a series of campaigns, in which he displayed extraordinary personal valor and high military genius, he overthrew four Syrian generals, rededicated the desecrated Temple of Jerusalem, and won religious freedom for his people. The war was renewed when the Syrian king appointed the apostate Jew Alcimus High Priest. Judas defeated the Syrian general at Adasa (in 161 B.C.); but a few weeks later, in an epic struggle against superior numbers, he himself was defeated and slain. Jewish independence was finally won under Simon, the last of the sons of Mathathias (in 142 B.C.).

2. The Doctrinal Books of the Old Testament

1. Hebrew Poetry.—Seven books of the Old Testament are classed as Doctrinal or Didactic. Five of them—*Job, Proverbs, Ecclesiastes, Wisdom,* and *Ecclesiasticus*—bear the special title of Wisdom Books, because it is their avowed purpose to instruct men in true Wisdom, to teach them "the true end of life and the right means to attain it." The Doctrinal Books are also called the *Poetical Books* of the Old Testament, because, with the exception of the introduction and the conclusion of *Job,* they are written in verse. Hebrew poetry knows neither meter nor rhyme. What distinguishes it from prose is a certain symmetry or balance of thought and expression between the members of a sentence or even of a long passage; "rhythm of sentences and ideas," as it has been aptly called. This characteristic is known as *Parallelism.* The Hebrew poet does not express a thought in *one* sentence, but in two or more parallel sentences.

2. Kinds of Parallelism.—Sometimes the poet expresses the same idea in different words in the several parts of the sentence, as in Job 20,4f.:

"This I know from the beginning,
   since man was placed upon the earth,
That the praise of the wicked is short,
   and the joy of the hypocrite but for a moment."

Sometimes the thought contained in the first part of the verse is confirmed by contrasting it with its opposite in the second part, as in Proverbs 15,1 :

"A mild answer breaketh wrath,
   but a harsh word stirreth up fury."

Or the thought expressed in the first verse is developed, proved or illustrated in the succeeding verse or verses, as in the well-known lines of Ecclesiastes, 12,1 :

"Remember thy Creator in the days of thy youth,
   before the time of affliction come,
And the years draw nigh of which thou shalt say :
   'They please me not.' "

Occasionally the three kinds of parallelism are combined in the same passage, which adds to the beauty and variety of the poem.

A few Hebrew poems, such as the *Lamentations* of the Prophet Jeremias, have the *alphabetical form,* the successive verses beginning with the successive letters of the Hebrew alphabet. This arrangement is not discernible in the English translation, except that in the *Lamentations* the Hebrew letter name is prefixed to each verse.

A more or less brief characterization of each of the Doctrinal Books must suffice.

3. The Book of Job is a literary masterpiece which takes rank among the great classics of all time. Job, the hero of the book, is an historical character, but the book itself is a didactic poem in which are embedded lyrical passages of fascinating beauty. In the form of a dialogue, preceded by a prologue and followed by an epilogue in prose, it treats of the problem of suffering, seeking the answer to the question : How can the afflictions of the innocent be reconciled with the justice of God ?

Job lived in the land of Hus, on the borders of the Syrian Desert. Though not an Israelite, he worships the true God. His prosperity and greatness correspond to his piety, for he is "simple and upright, and fearing God, and avoiding evil."

Satan claims that Job's piety is selfish, the natural return for his unexampled prosperity, and boasts that if stripped of his possessions he will curse God to His face. God permits Satan to put him to the test, first by depriving him of his children and his wealth in herds of sheep and cattle and camels; then by striking him with the terrible scourge of leprosy. Job stands the test triumphantly: "The Lord gave," he says, "and the Lord hath taken away: blessed be the name of the Lord."

JOB IN HIS ADVERSITY

The youthful Eliu, the son of Barochel the Buzite, defending Job against his accusers.

His wife also tempts him. She is firmly convinced of his innocence, but wavers in her trust in God, whom she accuses of punishing her husband unjustly. "Curse God, and die!" is her advice to Job. "We have received good things at the hand of God, why not evil?" he replies, and this temptation is also disposed of.

Being a leper, Job has to live apart from his fellow-men. His abode is a garbage-heap on the outskirts of the village. A makeshift roof supported by four rods is his only protection against the burning rays of the sun. Hearing of his great misfortune, his old friends Eliphaz, Baldad, and Sophar, come to condole with him—but in their own fashion. Evidently, they say, Job must be a great sinner, otherwise God would not have punished him: let him repent of his sins, and all will be well with him. But Job's conscience does not reproach him with crime. He therefore continues to protest his innocence, while at the same time upholding the justice of God. The debate runs through twenty-nine chapters. In the end Job disavows under solemn oath all the offenses charged against him by his friends, so that, in his case, their contention that all suffering is a punishment for sin, does not hold. There must be some other cause for suffering besides sin.

At this point a new champion enters the lists. The youthful Eliu, who had been an intensely interested but silent observer of the debate, reminds the four old men that suffering may be sent by God as a means of *probation* and *purification* for higher glory. The just man is tried by affliction as gold by fire.

While Eliu is yet speaking, "the air suddenly thickens into clouds," and God Himself, to whom Job had repeatedly appealed, appears in the storm-wind. He does not solve the problem of suffering for the disputants, but in two grandiose speeches He gives them a *practical standard* by which to shape their conduct. Man cannot comprehend the power and wisdom of the Creator and Ruler of the universe. Hence, in affliction and suffering he should bend humbly and trustingly under the hand of the Almighty. In his first answer Job evades the question with the promise to be silent in future; but in his second answer he makes open confession of his mistakes and does penance in dust and ashes.

God severely reprimands Job's friends for their unjust accusations against him, calls Job "His servant" and a "just man," and at his request pardons the folly and injustice of his friends. Job's goods are restored to him twofold, and he dies at a good old age.

4. The Book of Proverbs is a collection of wise sayings, short discourses and parables in praise of true Wisdom. The folly of sin, which is the deadly enemy of Wisdom, and its dire consequences are painted in vivid colors, and all men are called upon to lead God-fearing lives—the only means of attaining happiness. A few examples will show what a wealth of wisdom is often contained in a single sentence:

"Go to the ant, O sluggard,
  consider her ways,
and learn wisdom." (6,6).

"The patient man is better than the valiant,
  And he that ruleth his spirit, than he that taketh cities." (16,32).

"To speak a word in due time,
  is like apples of gold on beds of silver." (25,11).

"Favor is deceitful, and beauty is vain:
  the woman that feareth the Lord, she shall be praised." (31,30).

5. The Book of Ecclesiastes (i.e., the Preacher) discusses the problem: *What value has this earthly life for man?* Regarded from the viewpoint of the pessimist, this earthly life has no value.

All is vanity. All human endeavor is a "pursuing of the wind." There is an eternal sameness in things. There is nothing new under the sun. Gold and silver, the pleasures of the senses, the pleasures of the mind—all are vain, and produce nothing but "vexation of spirit." But the pessimist is wrong. There is another aspect to life. Man can be relatively happy. Therefore let him enjoy life and the good things which it offers; but let him ever be mindful of his end; let him "Fear God, and keep His commandments: for this is all man; and all things that are done, [every hidden and secret thing] God will bring into judgment for every error, whether it be good or evil" (12,13-14).

6. The Book of Wisdom was written in the first century before Christ by a Greek-speaking Jew of Alexandria in Egypt. The Egyptian rulers from Ptolemy VIII to Cleopatra were not well-disposed towards the Jews. The Jewish religion was despised by the powerful, the wealthy and the learned, and the faith of the Jews was in constant danger from idolatry and false philosophy. To strengthen the faith of his fellow countrymen, to console them in their afflictions, to raise their hearts above the sordidness and immorality by which they were surrounded—this is the purpose of the writer of the Book of Wisdom.

In the first part of the book (chs. 1-5) the author, in the person of Solomon, shows that Wisdom, that is, the ancient Jewish Religion, alone can give true happiness in this life and in the next. In the second part (chs. 6-19) he sings the praises of Wisdom and of the seeker after Wisdom, recommends prayer as the surest means of obtaining it, and describes its working in the history of the Israelites throughout the ages.

7. The author of **The Book of Ecclesiasticus** was Jesus, the son of Eleazar, of the family of Sirach. He was by profession a teacher of Wisdom in Jerusalem. Sirach wrote during the early decades of the second century before Christ, just prior to the Machabean wars. During this critical period of Jewish history, when the Chosen People were in danger of becoming hellenized and paganized, he stoutly champions the old religion and its Sacred Books, and shows how its lessons are applicable to every circumstance in life. In order to make his readers proud of being Jews, he eulogizes the heroes of Israel from Noe to Simon the High Priest.

The wealth of practical wisdom contained in Sirach's book won for it the honorable title of "The Ecclesiastical Book" and for its author the surname of "The Pedagogue." It appears to have been much used in the early Church as text-book for the instruction of the catechumens, or candidates for Baptism.

Ecclesiasticus was originally written in Hebrew. A grandson of the author translated it into Greek about the year 130 B.C.

8. The Psalms.—The Book of Psalms is a collection of 150 sacred hymns, which were sung to the accompaniment of the psaltery or lyre at the services in the Temple. The book is also known as the *Psalter of David,* because 73 Psalms bear his name and the rest are written in his spirit.

KING DAVID PRAISING GOD
A mural painting in the Monastery Church at Fahr, Switzerland.

Besides David, a number of other authors are mentioned in the Hebrew text: Moses, Solomon, the Levites Asaph, Eman and Ethan, and the sons of Core. Psalms which bear no author's name are called "orphan psalms."

The enumeration of the Psalms from Ps. 9 to Ps. 146 differs in the Hebrew and Greek texts. The Vulgate and the Douay Bible follow the Greek enumeration, while the Protestant versions adopt that of the Hebrew.

The Psalter is divided into five books. The first two contain older hymns mostly by King David; in the last three books there are many psalms composed during the Babylonian Captivity and shortly after the return of the exiles.

According to their theme, the Psalms are generally divided into six classes:

1. Psalms of *Prayer,* including Psalms of praise, thanksgiving, impetration and penitence.
2. *Didactic* or Moral Psalms, which give instruction on God and His Attributes, and on the relations of man to God.
3. *Historical* or National Psalms, which celebrate remarkable events in the history of the Chosen People.
4. *Festal* Psalms, especially the five known as the great *Hallel* (Pss. 112-117), which all begin with Alleluia, and were sung at the three great annual festivals; and the fifteen *gradual* Psalms (Pss. 119-133), which were sung on the Feast of Tabernacles by the singers of the Temple on the fifteen steps (*gradus*) leading up to the court of the priests.
5. *Maledictory* Psalms, in which the Psalmist calls down the punishment of God upon his enemies.
6. *Messianic* Psalms—Pss. 2, 15, 21, 44, 68, 71, 109—which contain prophecies regarding the Messias and His Kingdom.

No Old Testament book was quoted so often by Our Lord as the Psalms. He uses them to prove His Messiaship, and with a Psalm on His lips He expires on the Cross. It was therefore but natural that the Church should cherish them. She prescribes them for her public worship, and recommends them for private devotion. The Psalms form the main part of the Breviary, and the Introit, the Gradual, and the Offertory of the Mass are nearly always taken from them.

The Fathers of the Church are tireless in their praises of the Psalter. The Psalter, they assure us, is an abundant fountain of divine truths, a summary of all moral teaching, an inexhaustible storehouse of wisdom, a poem spiced with heavenly unction and designed to heal all the ills of the soul, a book in which wholesome doctrine and charm of diction are harmoniously combined; a book for all who wish to praise the majesty, the omnipotence, the wisdom and the providence of God, to plead with the Supreme Judge for mercy or to thank Him for favors received.

9. The Canticle of Canticles.—In the form of an allegory—

the love of Solomon for his bride, the shepherdess Sulamith—the
inspired poet sings of the love and fidelity of Jehovah towards His
Chosen People. Following the example of the Fathers, the Church
applies the contents of the book to describe the love of God for
His bride, the Church, and for all pious and God-fearing souls,
above all for the Immaculate Virgin. The Epistle for the Feast of
the Visitation, July 2, is taken from Cant. 2,8-14.

3. The Prophetical Books of the Old Testament

1. The Prophets of Israel.—The Prophets were men inspired
by God to "speak out His message" to mankind. They were the
religious leaders and teachers of Israel. It was their duty to stand
out against the wickedness of the rulers and the people, and to
lead the Israelites to a higher and purer knowledge and service
of God. About the time of Samuel (10 B.C.) the Prophets formed
a permanent institution, often living together in schools, in which
they prepared their pupils, who were called the "sons of the
Prophets," for their future calling. All the great prophets were
endowed with the power of foretelling the future and of working
miracles.

2. We distinguish two classes of Prophets: the **Older** and the
Younger Prophets. The older prophets delivered God's message
orally. Many of them were men of mighty deeds, such as Samuel,
Elias and Eliseus.

After reading the life-story of Samuel in the first book of Kings, we
cannot but see in him a "man of mighty spirit, rising far above his fellows;
a statesman with sane judgment who reads the signs of the times; a
prophet of Jehovah of majestic dignity and calm; in life as in death a ruler
of men and of kings."

The third book of Kings describes the fight to the death between the
prophets of Jehovah under the leadership of Elias and the cruel and
treacherous Jezabel, the Phoenician wife of King Achab of Israel, the
champion of the horridly immoral worship of Baal and Astaroth. Many of
the prophets have been slaughtered, and hundreds of them driven into exile.
Unmindful of the terrors of Jezabel, unaided and alone, Elias appears before
Achab, denounces the iniquities of his court, brings down the wrath of
God on the idolatrous nation, and in the memorable test by fire on Mount
Carmel vanquishes the priests of Baal and brings back the people to the
worship of the true God (3 Kings 17-20).

3. The Younger Prophets committed their messages to
writing. There are sixteen "writing prophets," twelve of whom,

because their writings are short, are known as the *Lesser Prophets*; the other four are called the *Greater Prophets*.

A number of *Prophetesses* are also mentioned in the Bible, among them Mary, the Sister of Moses, Debbora, who helped Barac, in the days of the Judges, to conquer the Chanaanites, and Holda,. who foretold to Josias the fall of the kingdom of Juda.

THE PROPHET ELIAS IN THE DESERT

The Four Greater Prophets

1. Isaias, the "king among the prophets," lived in the eighth century before Christ in the Kingdom of Juda. In the sixth chapter of his great book, Isaias describes his call to the prophetical office. In the Temple of Jerusalem the Lord, surrounded by Seraphim, appeared to him and commissioned him to proclaim the divine judgments on the sinful people and to exhort them to do penance. He was the friend and counselor of the pious King Ezechias, who was successful in all his undertakings as long as he listened to the Prophet's words. Isaias ended his glorious life by a glorious martyrdom, being sawed in two at the command of the wicked king Manasses, whose evil ways he had reproved.

ISAIAS AND HIS PROPHESIES ABOUT OUR SAVIOR
"Behold, a Virgin shall conceive, and bear a Son, and His name shall be called Emmanuel." (Isaias 7,14.)

The Book of Isaias falls naturally into two parts. The first part (chs. 1-35), appropriately called the "Book of Woes," contains the Prophet's repeated summons to Juda and Israel to do penance, and his prediction of the disasters that should overtake them if they did not return to God.

An historical appendix to the first part (chs. 36-39) describes the siege of Jerusalem under the Assyrian King Sennacherib, the miraculous delivery of the city, and the sickness and recovery of Ezechias.

In the second part (chs. 40-66), the "Book of Comfort," the Prophet foretells the deliverance of the people from the Babylonian Captivity and the establishment of the eternal Messianic kingdom of peace by the "Servant of Jehovah," the promised Redeemer.

St. Jerome calls Isaias the Evangelist of the Old Testament, because he depicted so faithfully the earthly life, passion and death of the Messias (chs. 52-53). The Advent liturgy contains many passages from Isaias.

2. Jeremias himself tells us how, in the thirteenth year of the reign of the pious King Josias (640-609), when he was still young and inexperienced, he was called to be a prophet to his people (1,4-19). He was commanded by God to warn the people of the coming destruction of Jerusalem, and to counsel them to meet the judgments of Jehovah with contrite hearts. In spite of many disappointments, persecutions and failures, Jeremias devoted nearly fifty years of his life to his sacred calling. Like a "fortified

THE PROPHET JEREMIAS
After the Sculpture in the Sixtine Chapel

city, a pillar of iron and a wall of brass," he opposed the idolatry and immorality of the princes and the people. Repeated attempts were made upon his life. Once he was placed in the stocks for twenty-four hours. When he predicted the destruction of the Temple, the priests demanded his life as a traitor. King Joachin (608-598) tossed his prophecies into the fire and ordered the prophet and his secretary Baruch to be imprisoned. Jeremias concealed himself, and from his place of hiding continued to pour forth denunciations and warnings. He tried to dissuade Sedecias (597-588) from his foolhardy rebellion against the mighty King Nabuchodonosor of Babylon, but his efforts were rewarded with imprisonment. Nabuchodonosor himself set him free in 588 B.C.

After the destruction of Jerusalem and the Temple, Jeremias composed his *Lamentations,* in which he describes the miseries of the people and the devastation of the Holy City. In her Good Friday liturgy the Church puts into the mouth of the suffering Savior the words of the third chapter of the Lamentations.

According to a Jewish tradition Jeremias was stoned to death by the Jews with whom he had retired into Egypt. Jeremias was a special figure of Christ in the ignominy and persecutions to which he was subjected, and in his charity for his persecutors.

3. The Prophecy of **Baruch,** the disciple and secretary of Jeremias, is placed in the Bible after the prophecy of his master. Baruch was transported to Babylon, and here he composed a confession of Israel's guilt before God. In four poems, each beginning with the words: "Be of good heart," he announces the speedy return of the exiles to Jerusalem. The *Communion* for the 2nd Sunday of Advent is taken from this prophecy.

4. Ezechiel, of priestly family, was among the captives that were carried away to Babylon in the year 597 B.C. He is called "The Prophet of Divine Fidelity," because he emphasizes the fact that God is faithful in His threats as well as in His promises. He kept up the courage of his fellow-captives by foretelling the doom of Babylon, the end of the captivity, and the redemption of mankind by the Messias. He, too, is said to have ended his days by martyrdom. The symbols of the four Evangelists are taken from the vision recounted in the first chapter of his prophecy.

5. Daniel was of the royal blood of the kings of Juda. With the noblest of the Jews he was taken as a captive to Babylon in

THE VISION OF THE PROPHET EZECHIEL

". . . when I was in the midst of the captives by the river Chobar, the heavens were opened, and I saw the visions of God." (Ezechiel 1,1.)

606 B.C. He stood in high favor with the Babylonian kings and with **Cyrus,** the conqueror of Babylon. His importance lies in the fact that he made the true God known to the pagans, prepared the deliverance of the Jews from captivity, and kept alive amongst them the hope of the Redeemer to come. We know nothing about his death. Tradition says that he was buried in Susa.

The most famous prophecies of Daniel are those concerning the "Son of Man" (7,13-14) and the date of the death of the Messias (9,22-27). The book of Daniel contains the well-known stories of the three young men in the fiery furnace, Nabuchodonosor's dream, Baltassar's vision (*Mane, Thecel, Phares*), Daniel in the lions' den, Susanna, and Bel and the dragon.

THE LESSER PROPHETS

1. The Prophets **Osee** and **Amos** foretold the destruction of the Kingdom of Israel. **Jonas** and **Nahum** prophesied the fall of the great city of Ninive. Jonas prefigured in his own person the death, burial and resurrection of Christ (Matt. 12,40). He was the only one among the Prophets sent to preach to the Gentiles.

THE PROPHET DANIEL
From the Sculpture in the Sixtine Chapel
"I beheld therefore in the vision of the night, and lo, one like
the Son of man came with the clouds of heaven." *From the
Prophecies by Daniel (7,13.)*

Abdias predicted the defeat and punishment of the Edomites;
Habacuc, the fall of Juda and Babylon; **Joel, Micheas** and
Sophonias the punishment of the Israelites for their sins.
Micheas foretold that Christ should be born in Bethlehem (5,2;
See Matt. 2,4).

2. Aggeus and **Zacharias** prophesied after the Babylonian
Captivity. Aggeus was sent by the Lord to exhort Zorobabel to
finish the building of the second Temple. He assured him that
this second Temple should be more glorious than the first, because
the Messias should honor it with His presence. Zacharias prophesied in the same year as Aggeus and upon the same occasion. He
foretold the triumphal entry of Jesus into Jerusalem on Palm
Sunday, the treason of Judas, and the passion and death of Christ.

3. Malachias was the last of the Prophets before John the
Baptist and lived about four hundred years before the birth of

Christ. He foretold the coming of Christ and His precursor, the reprobation of the Jews and their sacrifices, the calling of the Gentiles, and the institution of the Sacrifice of the Mass, the "clean oblation" that was to be offered up in every place "from the rising of the sun even to the going down" (1,10-11).

SUGGESTIONS FOR STUDY AND REVIEW

1. Run through the Gospel of St. Matthew and note down the books of the Old Testament quoted by him. You will find the references in the footnotes to the Gospel.
2. In what books of the Bible would you look for the following well-known stories: Fall of our first parents, the Deluge, the Tower of Babel, Joseph and his brethren, the Plagues of Egypt, the Golden Calf, the Manna, the Fall of Jericho, Jephte's Daughter, David and Saul, the Queen of Sheba, the Archangel Raphael, the Jewish Queen of Persia, Judas Machabeus?
3. Copious extracts in the words of the Bible, from all the books of the Old Testament will be found in Hald, *Readings from the Bible,* and Eaton, *The Bible Beautiful.*
4. Annotate the following: *Pentateuch, Decalogue, Feast of Purim, Parallelism, Wisdom Books, Orphan Psalms, Messianic Psalms, Psalter, Prophet, "Writing Prophets," Lamentations, "Son of Man," The "Last of the Prophets," The "King among the Prophets."*

CHAPTER V

Sources of Faith: Holy Scripture—(Continued)

C. THE BOOKS OF THE NEW TESTAMENT

1. The Historical Books of the New Testament

1. Gospel and Gospels.—There are five historical books in the New Testament: the Gospels of *Matthew, Mark, Luke,* and *John,* and the *Acts of the Apostles.* The word Gospel means "glad tidings," or good news (Anglo-Saxon *god,* good, and *spel,* tale, recital) concerning Christ, the Kingdom of God, and salvation. "And Jesus went about all Galilee, teaching in their synagogues, and preaching the *gospel* of the kingdom" (Matt. 4,23). Hence the word was very properly applied to the history of the life and teachings of Christ. The writers of the Gospels are called *Evangelists,* from the Greek word for good news—*euangelion.*

The Gospels of Matthew, Mark, ana Luke are called the *Synoptic Gospels,* because of their many agreements in matter, arrangement, and language (Greek, *synopsis,* which means "presenting or taking a common view of anything").

The Gospel was at first propagated *orally,* and it was everywhere the same. Later on when it was committed to writing, it was still spoken of as the *one* Gospel, but distinguished as the Gospel "according to" Matthew, Mark, Luke and John. There were other accounts of the deeds and words of Jesus (Luke 1,1), but these four alone were received by the Church into her *Canon* as inspired.

2. St. Matthew was a Galilean. He was known originally as Levi. As tax-gatherer at Capharnaum, he collected customs duties for King Herod. Although a Jew, he was despised by the Pharisees, who hated all publicans, as the tax-collectors were called. One day while he was sitting in the custom house, Jesus passed by and said to him: "Follow Me." Matthew immediately arose and followed Him and made a great feast for Him in his house. He accompanied Jesus up to the time of His Passion, and was one of the witnesses of His Resurrection and Ascension. According to a very old tradition he suffered martyrdom whilst preaching the Gospel to the pagans south of the Caspian Sea.

CHRIST AND THE FOUR EVANGELISTS

"Be mindful that the Lord Jesus Christ is risen again from the dead, of the seed of David, according to my gospel." (II. Tim. 2,8.)

43

St. Matthew wrote his Gospel in Hebrew (Aramaic) before the year 70 A.D. The Hebrew original is lost; we have, however, the Greek translation made either by St. Matthew himself or by one of his contemporaries. St. Matthew's aim is to show how Jesus of Nazareth fulfilled the prophecies of the Old Testament concerning the Messias. His symbol is a winged man, because he begins his Gospel with the human ancestry of Christ.

3. St. Mark, also called John Mark, was a native of Jerusalem. His mother's house was a meeting-place for the Apostles and their disciples. He accompanied St. Paul on his first missionary journey, but returned to Jerusalem before it was ended. Ten years later he was with St. Paul in Rome. For some years he was the companion of St. Peter. According to a later tradition, St. Mark founded the Church of Alexandria in Egypt. He wrote his Gospel for the Christians of Rome, who wished to have a synopsis of St. Peter's preaching. The lion, the dweller in the desert, is the symbol of St. Mark, because he begins his Gospel with the mission of St. John the Baptist, "the voice of one crying in the wilderness."

4. St. Luke, a Greek of Antioch, was by profession a physician. After his conversion he became the friend and companion of St. Paul, whom he accompanied on his second missionary journey from Troas to Philippi, and on his third from Greece to Asia Minor. He was with St. Paul during his two years' captivity in Caesarea and accompanied him to Rome. Here, it seems, he wrote his Gospel for a distinguished citizen named Theophilus, in order to instruct him in the life and doctrine of Christ. He was alone with St. Paul at the time of the great Apostle's last imprisonment.

We owe to St. Luke many details about St. John the Baptist. Our Lady, and the early life of Our Lord not given by the other Evangelists. Several of the most beautiful parables of Our Lord are found only in St. Luke: the Good Samaritan, the Prodigal Son, the Unjust Steward, the Rich Man and Lazarus, the Pharisee and the Publican. The ox, a sacrificial animal, is the emblem of St. Luke, because he begins his Gospel with the story of the priest Zachary offering a sacrifice in the Temple.

5. St. John, the Beloved Disciple, was the son of the Galilean fisherman Zebedee, and Salome, one of the pious women who followed Jesus to the Cross. His brother was James the Elder, his home-town probably Bethsaida. He was originally a disciple of St. John the Baptist, and, with St. Andrew, the first of the Apostles to follow Christ. He and his brother received from Christ the surname "Boanerges," that is, "sons of thunder." With Peter and James he belonged to the favorite Apostles of the Lord. At the Last Supper he leaned his head on Our Lord's bosom. He followed His Master to the foot of the Cross and received His last will: "Woman, behold thy son; Son, behold thy Mother."

After the Descent of the Holy Ghost, St. John labored with St. Peter in Jerusalem and Samaria. He seems to have remained in Jerusalem until the death of the Blessed Virgin. He then went to Ephesus and became the head of all the Churches of Asia Minor. Under the Emperor Domitian he was cast into a cauldron of boiling oil and later exiled to the island of Patmos. After the death of Domitian he returned to Ephesus, where he died about the year 100 A.D.

St. John wrote his Gospel in his old age to prove against the heretics of his time that Jesus is the Son of God. He quotes chiefly those discourses of Christ from which His divinity can be most clearly proved. The eagle, which soars highest of all birds, is the symbol of St. John, who, in the first words of his Gospel, carries us to Heaven itself: "In the beginning was the Word, and the Word was with God, and the Word was God."

6. The **Acts of the Apostles.**—The *Acts* (i.e., "deeds") were written by St. Luke towards the end of the first captivity of St. Paul in Rome about 62 A.D. The book is dedicated to Theophilus, the same friend to whom St. Luke dedicated his Gospel.

The *Acts of the Apostles* relates: (1) the history of the early Church in Jerusalem and Antioch, and the history of St. Peter till the year 42, when he left Jerusalem; (2) the history of St. Paul till his captivity in Rome in the year 61.

2. The Doctrinal Books of the New Testament

1. The Epistles of St. Paul.—Of the fourteen Epistles of St. Paul, the two to the *Thessalonians* were written on his second Missionary Journey from Corinth (A.D. 50-52). During his third Missionary Journey he wrote the Epistle to the *Galatians*, the two Epistles to the *Corinthians*, and the Epistle to the *Romans* (A.D. 53-58). During his first captivity in Rome he wrote to the *Philippians*, the *Colossians*, the *Ephesians* and to *Philemon* (A.D.

THE APOSTLE ST. PAUL

61-63). During his fourth Missionary Journey he wrote the *First Epistle to Timothy* and the Epistle to *Titus* (A.D. 64-66). During his second captivity in Rome, shortly before his martyrdom, he wrote the *Second Epistle to Timothy* (A.D. 66-67). It is not known when the Epistle to the *Hebrews* was written. In our Bible the Epistles are arranged as follows:

1. The Epistles to whole Churches, first the longer ones, then the shorter ones;
2. The Epistles to private persons;
3. The Epistle to the Hebrews.

All the epistles of St. Paul are written more or less on the same plan. They contain a doctrinal and a moral section, with an introduction and a conclusion. St. Paul usually dictated his epistles to a secretary; only the greetings at the end were written with his own hand as a proof of their genuineness. The epistles to the Galatians and to Philemon he seems to have written himself. All the epistles were written on special occasions and to meet special needs, but each one reflects the keen and noble character of the Apostle and gives a deep insight into the sublime mysteries of the Faith.

2. The Catholic Epistles.—The New Testament Epistles not written by St. Paul are called *Catholic Epistles*. Only two of the seven are addressed to particular persons; the rest are intended, it would seem, for groups of Christian communities in Palestine or Asia Minor.

The author of the **Epistle of James** is the Apostle St. James the Less, who because of his kinship with Christ is called the "Brother of the Lord," and who had been appointed by his brother-apostles first Bishop of Jerusalem. It is addressed to the Jewish Christians living outside of Palestine. The exhortation not to be satisfied with merely hearing the word of God, but to live the faith by means of good works, is the main theme of the Epistle. It also contains the counsel for the sick "to summon the priests of the Church to pray over them, and to anoint them with oil in the name of the Lord" (5,14-15).

In the **First and Second Epistles of Peter,** the Prince of the Apostles warns the faithful against conforming to the pagan spirit by which they are surrounded, and exhorts them to fidelity to their Christian calling in spite of persecution.

Of the three **Epistles of John,** the first is closely related to the Fourth Gospel. It is addressed to no particular Church, preaches faith in Christ, the Son of God, as the means of attaining eternal life, and urges the Christians to practice charity. The *Second Epistle* is addressed to a high-born Christian lady and her children. The Apostle admonishes his friends to practice brotherly love, and warns them against certain false teachers who denied the Incarnation. In the *Third Epistle* St. John commends the faith of a certain Gaius and praises him for his hospitality towards traveling missionaries.

St. Jude, also called Judas Thaddeus, the brother of St. James the Less, is the author of the epistle that bears his name. It was written before the year 63, probably in Palestine, and addressed to Jewish converts. In strong language the Apostle warns his readers against the machinations of certain false teachers. The Epistle concludes with the following beautiful *doxology*, or short hymn of praise to God:

"Now to Him who is able to preserve you without sin, and to present you spotless before the presence of His glory with exceeding joy, in the coming of Our Lord Jesus Christ to the only God Our Savior, through Jesus Christ Our Lord, be glory, and magnificence, empire and power, before all ages, and now, and for all ages of ages. Amen."

3. The Prophetical Book of the New Testament:
The Apocalypse of St. John

The Apocalypse, or Book of Revelations of St. John, is the only prophetical book of the New Testament. It contains the visions which St. John saw during his exile on the island of Patmos in the year 95 or 96. When St. John wrote the Apocalypse, the Christians were being hunted down, imprisoned and put to death for their Faith. It was the Apostle's purpose to strengthen their courage by foretelling the final downfall of their Roman persecutors and the victory of the kingdom of Christ. In the last two chapters the glories of the New Jerusalem, the kingdom of the Church Triumphant, are painted in gorgeous colors. Thus, the *last* book of Holy Scripture holds out to us the joyful hope of one day obtaining possession of the heavenly paradise, while the *first* book (Genesis) tells us how the earthly paradise was lost by the sin of our first parents.

SUGGESTIONS FOR STUDY AND REVIEW

1. What two meanings are attached to the word "Gospel"?
2. Why do we speak of the Gospel according to St. Matthew, etc.?
3. Why are the first three Gospels called the Synoptic Gospels?
4. Look up the following texts: Matt. 9,9-14; Mark 2,14-17; Acts 12,12; Col. 4,10; Acts 12,26; Acts 13,13; Acts 15,37-39; Phil. 1,24; Acts 16,10ff.; Col. 4,14; 2 Tim. 4,11. What do you learn from these passages about the writers of the first three Gospels?
5. Where would you look for an account of the conversion and apostolic labors of St. Paul?
6. Which is the longest and which the shortest book of the New Testament?
7. Do you think that the Gospels contain a complete account of all that Christ did during His life on earth? See John 20,30, and 21,25.
8. *Reading:* Joseph Beck, *The Beauty of Holy Scripture* (a Paulist Pamphlet, The Paulist Press, N. Y.).

CHAPTER VI

Sources of Faith: Tradition

"Hold the traditions which you have learned."—2 THESS. 2,14.

I. MEANING AND NECESSITY OF TRADITION

1. What Tradition Means.—Our Lord did not command His Apostles to *write,* but to *teach.* "Going, therefore, teach ye all nations . . . to observe all things whatsoever I have commanded you" (Matt. 28,19). The Apostles told their disciples *orally* what their Divine Master had communicated to them. "The things which thou hast *heard* of me by many witnesses," St. Paul writes to Timothy, "the same commend (i.e., tell) to faithful men, who shall be fit to *teach* to others also" (2 Tim. 2,2).

Most of the truths which the Apostles preached at the command of Christ were afterwards written down by the Apostles themselves or by some of their disciples. But many important truths continued to be handed down by word of mouth. In fact, in the whole New Testament we cannot find any sign of a purpose to put on paper all that Christ revealed. St. John, the last of the Apostles to write, says expressly that he has recounted only a part of what Christ had done: "Many other signs also did Jesus in the sight of His disciples, which are not written in this book" (20,30). And St. Paul writes to the Thessalonians: "Brethren, hold the traditions which you have learned, whether by *word* or by our epistle" (2 Thess. 2,14). *It is these truths, precepts, and counsels, revealed by God, but not found in the Written Word of God, that we call Tradition.*

2. Scripture and Tradition of Equal Value.—Since the truths contained in Scripture and those handed down by Tradition both come from God, Scripture and Tradition are of equal value as sources of faith. Both deserve the same reverence and respect. Each alone is sufficient to establish a truth of our holy faith.

The contents of Scripture and Tradition are not distinct from each other or alien to each other. But Tradition can *a*) contain a revealed truth not found in Scripture, or

b) explain more clearly and definitely a doctrine less clearly expressed in Scripture, e.g., the Immaculate Conception.

3. Necessity of Tradition.—The Bible nowhere tells us how many inspired books there are. If we did not know this for certain from Tradition, we should not even have a Bible. When Protestants appeal to Scripture against the Catholic Church, "they forget that it is from this very Church, and on her authority, that Scripture is received."

If we consulted the Bible only, we should still have to keep holy the Sabbath Day, that is, Saturday, with the Jews, instead of Sunday; we should have to abstain from eating things strangled and from blood (Acts 15,20); we should let little children die without Baptism, because, according to the mere words of the Bible text (Matt. 28,19), Christ gave the command first to teach, and then to baptize; we should not know that any man, or woman, or child that has attained the age of reason can validly baptize; we should not know the exact rite of validly administering each particular sacrament.

The Bible does not, in doubtful passages, decide upon the true meaning of its words; this Tradition does for us. All sects appeal to the Bible to prove their contradictory doctrines, and each one of them pretends to have hit upon its true meaning.

Thus we see that *Tradition is necessary*, and that *the Christian must believe all that God has revealed and the Church proposes to his belief, whether it be contained in Holy Scripture or in Tradition.*

4. The Catholic Rule of Faith.—Scripture and Tradition are called the *remote rule of faith*, because the Catholic does not base his faith *directly* on these sources. The *proximate rule of faith* is for him the One, Holy, Catholic, and Apostolic Church, which alone has received from God the authority to interpret infallibly the doctrines He has revealed, whether these be contained in Scripture or in Tradition.

2. THE RECORDS OF TRADITION

1. Where the Traditions Are Recorded.—The truths handed down by the Apostles by word of mouth were in the course of time committed to writing. These written records of Tradition can be found *a*) In the *Decrees of Popes and Councils.*

b) In the *Liturgical Books* of the Church.

c) In the *Inscriptions* on ancient tombs and public monuments which show what the early Church believed regarding the souls of the departed, intercessory prayer, the use of images, relics, etc.

d) In the genuine *Acts of the Martyrs,* which were written during the era of the persecutions and contain accounts of the trials of the Christians and of the truths which they professed and sealed with their blood.

e) In the works of the *Fathers of the Church.* The Fathers are the holy and learned writers of the early ages of Christianity. To those who were distinguished for extraordinary learning and purity of doctrine the Church gave the title of *Doctors.*

f) In the *Creeds* of the Church. Creed, from the Latin *credo,* "I believe," means either the entire body of beliefs held by the members of a particular religion, or a summary of the chief articles of faith professed by a church. In this latter sense we speak of the *four Creeds* of the Catholic Church:

   1. The *Apostles' Creed,* which goes back to the time of the Apostles and is used at Baptism and in the Breviary at the beginning of Matins and Prime and at the end of Compline.

   2. The *Nicene Creed,* which is said or sung at Mass immediately after the Gospel on all Sundays and on feasts of Our Lord, the Blessed Virgin, the Apostles, Doctors, etc. It is longer than the Apostles' Creed and contains the doctrine of the divinity of Christ and of the Holy Ghost as defined by the Councils of Nice (325 A.D.) and Constantinople (381 A.D.) against the heretics Arius and Macedonius. The words, "of whose Kingdom there shall be no end," were added against a certain Marcellus of Ancyra, who denied that Christ's reign would continue after the last judgment. The word, *"Filioque"* (who proceedeth from the Father *and the Son*) was added in the fifth century in Spain and later used in the whole West.

   3. The *Athanasian Creed,* so called after the great Doctor of the Church, St. Athanasius, but probably not composed by him. It contains a remarkably clear statement of the doctrines of the Blessed Trinity and the Incarnation. It is recited in the Breviary at Prime on the minor Sundays after Epiphany and Pentecost and on Trinity Sunday.

   4. The *Creed of Pius IV,* known also as the "Profession of the Tridentine Faith," was published by Pope Pius IV in 1564. It is especially directed against Luther and the other heretics of the sixteenth century. In 1877 Pius IX added a paragraph on the Primacy and Infallibility of the Pope as defined by the Vatican Council (1870 A.D.). Pope Pius X in 1910 appended a solemn repudiation of the errors of Modernism.

Since the time of St. Cyprian (3rd cent.) the common Latin term for what we call a Creed is *Symbolum,* or token, "by which a man may be known and recognized as a Christian." The Apostles' Creed is called in Latin *Symbolum Apostolorum.*

FATHERS AND DOCTORS OF THE CHURCH

2. The Church, the Interpreter of Tradition.—Just as the Church is the only infallible interpreter of the Sacred Scriptures, so from her alone can we learn the true meaning of Tradition. She alone has received from God the authority and the guidance necessary to interpret infallibly *all* revelation.

SUGGESTIONS FOR STUDY AND REVIEW

1. What is meant by Tradition?
2. Mention three or four doctrines certainly revealed by God but not contained in the Bible.
3. Why must we believe Tradition as well as Holy Scripture?
4. Where are the teachings of Tradition to be found? In your Church History you will find details about the various Records of Tradition.
5. Can you write a brief paragraph on each of the following: *Remote Rule of Faith, Proximate Rule of Faith, Fathers of the Church, Creed, Nicene Creed?*
6. Why are the Creeds also called Symbols?
7. From whom are we to learn the true meaning of Tradition?
8. If a Protestant asserts that Christ wished to see His doctrine preserved and spread by *Scripture alone,* ask him or her the following questions:
   a) Why did not Christ Himself write down His doctrines?
   b) Why did He not command His Apostles: *"Write* the Gospel to all nations"?
   c) Why did not *all* the Apostles commit the teachings of Christ to writing?
   d) Why did the Apostles and Evangelists who wrote write so *late* and only upon special occasions?
   e) Why did not Christ command that everyone, or at least every Christian, should learn to read?
   f) Why did Divine Providence ordain that the art of printing should be invented so late, especially since before that invention it was utterly impossible for the vast majority of men to purchase a Bible?
9. *Reading:* Conway, *Question Box,* pp. 77-80, "Divine Tradition."

CHAPTER VII

Necessity and Qualities of Faith

"Without faith it is impossible to please God."—HEB. 11,6.

1. FAITH NECESSARY TO SALVATION

1. Everyone insists that we believe his word, and feels hurt if we do not. With more right than any man can God demand faith in His word. If we refuse to believe Him, we really tell Him that He is a deceiver. Our Lord says: "He that believeth not, shall be condemned" (Mark 16,16); and in another place: "He that doth not believe is already judged" (John 3,18). And St. Paul teaches that "without faith it is impossible to please God" (Heb. 11,6).

2. He who wishes to attain a definite end must above all things know that end and the means to reach it. Now our last end, as we have seen, is the possession of God in Heaven. But this end is supernatural, and the means to attain it are supernatural. Hence we can know neither the one nor the other by our natural powers of reasoning, but only by supernatural enlightenment; that is, by believing what God has told us. *Hence Faith is absolutely necessary to attain our last end.* "He that *believeth,* and is baptized, shall be saved; but he that believeth not, shall be condemned" (Mark 16,16).

3. By faith is not meant any faith, otherwise it would not have been necessary for Christ to teach a definite faith, nor could He have threatened with eternal punishment those who do not receive this faith. Hence the faith necessary to salvation can mean only the faith which Christ, the Son of God, taught mankind. By this faith alone, and by no other, we are made partakers of Christ, and without Christ there is no salvation. "For there is no other name under heaven given to men whereby we must be saved" (Acts 4,12). *It is therefore a grievous sin to say, or even to think, knowingly and willingly, that it does not matter what faith we profess.*

2. QUALITIES OF FAITH

God in His goodness has given us the grace of the true faith. But this faith will not save us unless it is *universal, firm, living,* and *constant.*

1. Our Faith Must Be Universal.—God made many promises to Abraham. Abraham believed not only the one or the other, but all of them without exception; his faith was *universal.* God has revealed many truths to us. If we believe all these truths without exception, then our faith is *universal.*

Our faith is *universal* when we believe not only *some* but *all* the truths which God has revealed and which the Catholic Church proposes to our belief.

No one is at liberty to admit and believe only some of the teachings of Christ and His Church and to reject others. For,

1. Christ says: "Preach the Gospel to every creature; he that believeth not, shall be condemned" (Mark 16,15f.). And, again: "Teach them to observe *all* things whatsoever I have commanded you" (Matt. 28,20). And St. John writes: "Whosoever *revolteth,* and continueth not in the doctrine of Christ, hath not God" (2 John 1,9).

2. He who believes of the doctrine of Christ only what he pleases, has no faith at all, for he does not believe God, but his own private judgment.

3. He who rejects even one of the truths revealed by God, denies the truthfulness of God.

We must believe all the truths revealed by God. But that does not mean that each one of us must also *know* all the truths of faith. There are truths the knowledge of which is not *absolutely* necessary to salvation, and others which everyone, even the child that has attained the use of reason, must know in order to be saved. The truths which everyone ought to know explicitly are the following:

1. That there is *one* God, who created all things;
2. That God rewards the good and punishes the wicked;
3. That there are three Persons in God, the Father, the Son, and the Holy Ghost;
4. That the Second Person of the Blessed Trinity became man and redeemed us on the cross;
5. That the soul of man is immortal;
6. That the grace of God is necessary for salvation.

2. Our Faith Must Be Firm.—God told Zachary through the Angel Gabriel: "Thy prayer is heard, and thy wife Elizabeth shall bear thee a son" (Luke 1,13). Zachary answered: "Whereby shall I know this? for I am an old man, and my wife is advanced in years." He hesitated between the truth and its opposite. We say he *doubted*. His faith was not *firm*. Abraham's faith, on the contrary, was firm. God had promised to make him the father of a great nation, and he did not doubt God's word even when God asked him to sacrifice his only son Isaac.

THE ANGEL GABRIEL AND ZACHARY

"And there appeared to him an angel of the Lord, standing on the right side of the altar of incense. And Zachary seeing him was troubled and fear fell upon him. But the angel said to him: Fear not, Zachary, for thy prayer is heard: and thy wife Elizabeth shall bear thee a son, and thou shalt call his name John. (Luke 1,11-13.)

Our faith is *firm* when we believe without the least doubt. Our faith *must* be firm; for whoever doubts willfully, thinks that God can deceive or be deceived. Even to suppose the possibility of such a thing is a grave offense against God. God punished Moses, Aaron and Zachary on account of a doubt.

3. Our Faith Must Be Living.—God has revealed to us what we must do or not do; for example: "Thou shalt honor thy father and mother."—"Thou shalt not steal." What God commands is good; what He forbids is evil. If we avoid the evil which God forbids, and do the good which He commands, we live in the manner our faith prescribes, and then our faith is *lively*, or living.

Living up to the faith which we profess, that is, performing *good works*, this is the only true proof that our faith is alive. "As the body without the spirit is dead," says St. James, "so also faith without works is dead" (James 2,26). Faith without good works cannot save us, neither can good works without faith. But it must be remembered that good works, such as are necessary for salvation, can only be performed by one who is in possession of *sanctifying grace*; that is, by one who loves God in his heart. "In Christ Jesus neither circumcision availeth anything, nor uncircumcision, but *faith that worketh by charity*" (Gal. 5,6). "And if I should have all faith, so that I could remove mountains, and have not charity [that is, love of God, sanctifying grace], I am nothing" (1 Cor. 13,2).

4. Our Faith Must Be Constant.—The pagans did all in their power to make the Christians renounce the faith. They promised them riches and honors if they denied Christ; they threatened them with the most dreadful tortures and even death itself if they refused to do so. But the martyrs were ready to lose all, even life, rather than fall away from the faith. Their faith was *constant*.

5. Many are the dangers to our faith: among the gravest are the following:

1. Pride and excessive reasoning on the mysteries of our holy religion;
2. Neglect of prayer and of the other religious duties;
3. Worldliness and a wicked life;
4. Reading books or other literature that is hostile to the faith;
5. Intercourse with scoffers at religion;
6. Mixed marriages;
7. Joining societies forbidden by the Church.

SUGGESTIONS FOR STUDY AND REVIEW

1. Give examples showing how faith is rewarded by God. See Matt. 8,13 and 15,28; Mark 9,16-26.
2. Can you name half a dozen famous converts to the true faith? How were they converted? Consult the *Catholic Encyclopedia*.
3. In order to be prepared to answer objections brought against the Catholic doctrine that whoever will be saved must belong to the *one, true* Church, ponder well the following propositions:
   a) "Whoever, *through his own grievous fault,* fails to become a member of the Catholic Church, cannot be saved."
   b) "Whoever, *without his fault,* is not a Catholic, but sincerely seeks the truth and keeps the commandments of God to the best of his knowledge, does not belong to the visible body of the Church, but belongs to her soul, and therefore receives from God sanctifying grace and can be saved."*
4. Why is the privilege of belonging to the Catholic Church a grace for which we can never thank God enough? (See No. 7.)
5. Prepare a short paper to be read or delivered before the class, on the following topic: "Our Faith Must Be Universal, Firm, Living, and Constant."
6. Copy the following texts: Matt. 11,25; Matt. 21,43; 1 Tim. 1,19; Matt. 7,15; Gal. 5,9. Show how these texts explain the loss of faith.
7. *Reading:* Stoddard, *Rebuilding a Lost Faith,* Ch. XXII, "Some Catholic Privileges."

---

* Since the publication of the encyclical *Mystici Corporis* (1943), theologians recognize that it is better to speak of such persons as belonging to the Church in an invisible manner, rather than as belonging only to her "soul." —*Editor,* 1990.

CHAPTER VIII

Profession of Faith. The Sign of the Cross.

"With the mouth confession is made unto salvation."—ROM. 10,10.

1. It is not sufficient to believe in our hearts; we must also profess our faith outwardly. "Everyone," says Our Lord, "that shall confess Me before men, I will also confess him before my Father who is in Heaven. But he that shall deny Me before men, I will also deny him before My Father who is in Heaven" (Matt. 10,32).

The most important thing about a clock is the works; but the works alone are not sufficient; the clock must also have hands, otherwise we shall never know what time it is. It is the same with faith. Faith must be in our hearts; that is all-important. But we must also make outward profession of it. "With the heart," says St. Paul, "we believe unto justice: but with the mouth, confession is made unto salvation" (Rom. 10,10).

2. We can profess our faith by word and deed. By *word*, like the three young men in the Book of Daniel, who declared: "Be it known to thee, O king, that we will not worship thy gods, nor adore the golden statue which thou hast set up" (3,18). Or like St. Peter, who, when Christ asked His disciples, "Whom do you say that I am?" replied: "Thou art Christ, the Son of the living God" (Matt. 16,15f.). By *deeds*, if we assist at Mass and at other divine services; if we receive the sacraments; if we genuflect, and fold our hands in prayer; if we make the sign of the cross reverently.

3. We use the Sign of the Cross to profess our faith, because it expresses the two principal mysteries of Christianity: the mystery of the Most Blessed Trinity and the mystery of the Redemption through the Incarnation, Passion and Death of Jesus Christ, the Son of God.

The Sign of the Cross devoutly made arms us against the snares of the devil, arouses sentiments of faith, hope and charity within us, helps us to conquer human respect, and draws down the blessings of Heaven upon us. Hence it is good and wholesome to make the Sign of the Cross frequently, as the first Christians did, especially when we rise and when we go to bed, before and after prayers, before every important undertaking, and in all temptations and dangers.

"God forbid," says St. Paul, "that I should glory, save in the cross of Our Lord Jesus Christ" (Gal. 6,14).

"At every step and movement," writes Tertullian at the end of the second century, "when we go in or out, when we dress or put on our shoes, at the bath, at the table, when lights are brought, when we go to bed, when we sit down, whatever it is which occupies us, we mark the forehead with the Sign of the Cross."—*On the Crown*, 3.

We usually make the Sign of the Cross on our forehead, mouth and heart, at the reading of the Gospel, in order that God through the merits of Christ Crucified may give us grace to understand the Gospel with our mind, to profess with our mouth, and to love it with our heart.

Cardinal Newman was still a member of the Anglican Church when he wrote the following beautiful lines on the efficacy of the Sign of the Cross:

> Whene'er across this sinful flesh of mine
>   I draw the Holy Sign,
> All good thoughts stir within me, and renew
>   Their slumbering strength divine;
> Till there springs up a courage high and true
>   To suffer and to do.
> And who shall say, but hateful spirits around,
>   For their brief hour unbound,
> Shudder to see, and wail their overthrow?
>   While on far heathen ground
> Some lonely Saint hails the fresh odor, though
>   Its source he cannot know.

4. We are not bound always and on all occasions to profess our faith openly, but we must do so whenever the honor of God, the spiritual good of our neighbor, or our own spiritual good requires it; for instance, when we are questioned in regard to our faith by someone who has the right to do so, we *must* confess our faith.

A solemn profession of faith must be made by converts on their reception into the Church, by bishops at their consecration and on their deathbed, by priests at their ordination, and by certain ecclesiastical officials when they assume office.

SUGGESTIONS FOR STUDY AND REVIEW

1. Must the faith be openly professed? if so, when? see Acts 4,20; Rom. 1,16.
2. Prepare a paper on "The Sign of the Cross," using the following questions for the disposition:

a) How do Catholics profess their faith?

b) Why do we use the Sign of the Cross to profess our faith?

c) How does the Sign of the Cross indicate the great mysteries of Christianity?

d) When should we make the Sign of the Cross?

e) Why is it good and wholesome frequently to make the Sign of the Cross?

f) Why do we make the Sign of the Cross on our forehead, mouth and heart at the reading of the Gospel?

g) What does Cardinal Newman say about the efficacy of the Sign of the Cross?

OUR LORD ON THE CROSS

ST. AUGUSTINE ON THE SIGN OF THE CROSS

"What but the Cross of Christ is the sign of Christ which everybody knows? Unless this Sign is set on the foreheads of believers, on the water whereby they are regenerated, on the chrism wherewith they are anointed, on the Sacrifice whence they are nourished, none of these things are rightly done."—Tract. 118,5 on St. John's Gospel.

SECTION II

CHIEF TRUTHS OF FAITH

Introduction

The chief truths which God has revealed and the Church proposes to our belief are summed up briefly in the **Apostles' Creed,** the most ancient of all the professions of faith.

The twelve articles of the Creed contain the mystery of the one God in three distinct Persons, the Father, the Son and the Holy Ghost, together with the actions attributed in a special manner to each of the Divine Persons.

The doctrine of the Most Blessed Trinity is divided into three principal parts, describing respectively:

1. The First Person of the Blessed Trinity and the Work of Creation (Art. 1);
2. The Second Person and the Mystery of Man's Redemption (Arts. 2-7);
3. The Third Person and the Work of Sanctification, which is begun here on earth by Grace and is to be perfected in Heaven by the Light of Glory (Arts. 8-12).

For easy reference we subjoin the text of the *Nicene Creed* together with that of the *Apostles' Creed*. The additions made by the Councils of Nice and Constantinople are printed in italics.

APOSTLES' CREED	NICENE CREED
I. I believe in God the Father Almighty, Creator of heaven and earth;	I believe in one God, the Father Almighty, Maker of heaven and earth, *and of all things visible and invisible.*
II. And in Jesus Christ, His only Son, Our Lord:	And in one Lord Jesus Christ, the only-begotten Son of God, *begotten of the Father before all ages; God of God, Light of Light, True God of True God; begotten, not made, consubstantial with the*

63

Father; by Whom all things
were made.

III. Who was conceived by the Holy Ghost, born of the Virgin Mary,

Who for us men, and for our salvation, came down from Heaven, and was incarnate by the Holy Ghost of the Virgin Mary: and was made man.

IV. Suffered under Pontius Pilate, was crucified, died and was buried.

He was crucified also for us, suffered under Pontius Pilate, and was buried.

V. He descended into hell; the third day He arose again from the dead.

And the third day He rose again according to the Scriptures, and

VI. He ascended into Heaven, sitteth at the right hand of God, the Father Almighty;

Ascended into Heaven. He sitteth at the right hand of the Father:

VII. From thence He shall come to judge the living and the dead.

And He shall come again with glory to judge the living and the dead; of Whose kingdom there shall be no end.

VIII. I believe in the Holy Ghost,

And I believe in the Holy Ghost, the Lord and Lifegiver, Who proceedeth from the Father and the Son, Who, together with the Father and the Son, is adored and glorified, Who spoke by the Prophets.

IX. The Holy Catholic Church, the Communion of Saints,

And in One, Holy, Catholic and Apostolic Church.

X. The forgiveness of sins,

I confess one Baptism for the remission of sins.

XI. The Resurrection of the Body, and

And I expect the Resurrection of the Dead,

XII. The Life Everlasting. Amen.

And the life of the world to come. Amen.

The twelve parts of the Creed are called *Articles* (from the Latin *articulus*, "a little joint") because they are connected with each other like joints of the body, and thus constitute one body of faith, or *one whole Creed*.

We should know the Creed, and recite it often. St. Ambrose advised his sister to say it every morning and every evening, and to look into it often during the day, as into a mirror. St. Augustine addressed the following words to his catechumens: "Receive, my dear children, this rule of faith which we call the *Symbol*, or Creed; engrave it on your hearts; carry it about always with you that it may be your defense, and that your memory may be an open book wherein you can read it continually."

The custom of saying the Creed frequently was one of the great means which the people of Ireland used to keep their faith alive during the long ages of persecution. It is still one of their favorite prayers.

SUGGESTIONS FOR STUDY AND REVIEW

1. Why is the summary of the chief truths of faith called the Creed? Apostles' Creed?
2. What do the twelve Articles of the Creed contain?
3. What are the differences between the Apostles' Creed and the Nicene Creed? Are any *new* doctrines contained in the Nicene Creed?
4. Why are the parts of the Creed called Articles?
5. Why should we say the Apostles' Creed frequently?
6. Why is the Creed said *after* the Gospel at Mass on Sundays?
7. What Articles of the Creed are commemorated by the Church on special Festivals?

CHAPTER I

Nature and Attributes of God

"I Am Who Am: . . . This is My Name forever." Ex. 3,14f.

I. THE NATURE OF GOD

1. Who God Is.—God is the infinitely perfect and absolutely simple Spirit, existing of Himself from all eternity; Creator of heaven and earth, and Sovereign Lord of all things.

In the Old Testament God is called: (*a*) *Elohim,* the infinitely great and glorious One; (*b*) *Adonai,* the Lord, and (*c*) *Jahve* (or Jehovah), He Who Is. After the Babylonian Captivity the Jews ceased to pronounce the name Jahve, and substituted Adonai for it. In the New Testament Christ tells us to call God by the name *Father.*

2. What the Scriptures Tell Us of God's Nature.—Since God is infinitely perfect, no created being can understand fully the nature of God. God is *incomprehensible.* He alone, as St. Paul says, "hath immortality, and inhabiteth light inaccessible, whom no man hath seen nor can see" (1 Tim. 6,16). Whatever we think or say of God must be directed by the revelations which He has made to us. Let us hear how God speaks of Himself in the Holy Scriptures.

a) When Moses received from God the commission to lead the children of Israel out of Egypt, he asked what answer he was to give, if the Israelites demanded by what authority he acted. "If they should say to me, What is His name? what shall I say to them?" God said to Moses, "*I Am Who Am.* Thus shalt thou say to the children of Israel: *He Who Is* hath sent me to you" (Ex. 3,13-14).

This revelation tells us in what the nature of God primarily consists. It tells us that God exists of Himself from all eternity. *He always was, He is, and always will be.* He is *self-existent*; all other beings owe their existence to Him.

b) In His conversation with the Samaritan woman at Jacob's well our Divine Savior said: "God is a spirit, and they that adore Him must adore Him in spirit and in truth" (John 4,24). Hence,

God, being a spiritual substance, has no body, nor the form, size, color or any other quality of bodies.

MOSES AND THE BURNING BUSH

"God said to Moses: I AM WHO AM. He said: Thus shalt thou say to the children of Israel: HE WHO IS, hath sent me to you." (Exod. 3,14.)

Holy Scripture speaks of God's eyes, ears, hands, etc., in order to help us to understand His attributes or perfections. The eyes and ears of God signify His omnipresence and omniscience; His arms signify His omnipotence; His heart is a symbol of His love and mercy.

When we say that God is a *spirit*, we do not mean that He is merely an abstraction, an idea; but we mean a *personal spirit*, a living intellectual spirit, free to will and to act. A *person* is a rational being which exists in itself and controls its own actions.

3. God and Human Reason.—Our reason can form an idea or notion of God by taking man, the highest creature of God on earth, as the starting point. We ascribe to God all the good qualities of man, we deny any imperfections in Him, and finally we extend all the good qualities of man beyond all limit. Thus: man is powerful; God is all-powerful. Man is good and kind; God is good and kind beyond compare. Our soul is made to the image and likeness of God. Hence it must in some way mirror the spirit of God; if it did not, we could never form any concept of God's nature.

2. ATTRIBUTES OR PERFECTIONS OF GOD

A. Attributes of the Divine Nature

Besides Self-existence, which is the fundamental attribute of God, the principal attributes of the Divine Nature are: *Immutability* (or Unchangeableness), *Eternity, Immensity* (and Omnipresence).

1. Unchangeableness.—Holy Scripture teaches us that God is unchangeable; that is, that neither He nor His decrees ever change. "God is not a man, that He should lie, nor as the son of man, that He should be changed" (Num. 23,19). "Thou foundedst the earth, and the heavens are the works of Thy hands. They shall perish, but Thou remainest; and all of them shall grow old like a garment. . . . But Thou art always the selfsame, and Thy years shall not fail" (Ps. 101,26-28). "With God there is no change, nor shadow of alteration" (James 1,17). A shadow is the slightest change that we know of, because it leaves no trace after it. Even this feeblest of all changes is denied of God by Scripture.

When we read in Scripture that "God repented" of having made man, or that God is angry, the phrases used are figurative and not to be taken literally. When God created the world, a change took place outside of Him, but not in Him, for His will, by which He created the world, is eternal. When God is said to hate a man if he sins, and to love him again if he repents, the change is not in God, but in the man. God's unchangeable nature does not operate in the same way in the soul of the sinner as in the soul of the just man. The same sun melts wax, whereas it hardens clay; it delights the healthy eye, but causes pain to the sick one.

2. Eternity.—When we speak of eternity, we deny all duration as measured by time. Time is of its very nature change, counted motion. Time began with the creation of the changeable world. God is eternal because He is unchangeable. For Him succession of time is replaced by an eternal present. *He is.* "I Am Who Am. . . . This is My name forever" (Ex. 3,14f.). God is the "eternal King," the "King of ages" (Tob. 13,6; 1 Tim. 1,17). "One day with the Lord is as a thousand years, and a thousand years as one day" (2 Pet. 3,8).

On account of our limited intelligence, we have to speak of a past and a future as well as of a present in God. We say: He always was and always will be. But in reality there is neither past nor future to God.

3. Immensity and Omnipresence.—Eternity denies time in regard to God; immensity denies space. God is measured neither by time nor space. Still, He is omnipresent in space since the creation of the world. "If heaven and the heavens of heavens cannot contain Thee, how much less this house which I have built?" says Solomon in his prayer at the dedication of the Temple (3 K. 8,27). And the Psalmist cries out in astonishment: "Whither shall I go from Thy spirit? or whither shall I flee from Thy face? If I ascend into Heaven, Thou art there. If I descend into Hell, Thou art present. If I take my wings early in the morning, and dwell in the uttermost parts of the sea, even there also shall Thy hand lead me, and Thy right hand shall hold me" (Ps. 138,7-10).

The omnipresent God is in the souls of the just, but also in the souls of sinners. "God is not far from every one of us," says St. Paul, "for in Him we live, and move, and are" (Acts 17,27f.). But the sinner does not permit the rays of God's grace to enlighten him. He is like a blind man in the sunshine.

B. Attributes of the Divine Intelligence

1. God Is All-Knowing.—God knows all things. He knows all that has existed or can exist, all that has been done or will be done or can be done. "The eyes of the Lord are far brighter than the sun, beholding round about all the ways of men, and the bottom of the deep, and looking into the hearts of men, into the most hidden parts; for all things were known to the Lord God before they were created; so also after they were perfected He beholdeth all things" (Ecclus. 23,28).

God also foresees the evil that men do, but men are not on that account forced to do evil. God foresees the evil deed because you do it; you do not do it because God foresees it.

But does not God know whether I shall go to Heaven or to Hell? Why, then, should I trouble about my salvation?

But God also foresees whether a field will bear a crop or not. If a farmer on that account would not plough and sow his field, God would foresee that his field bears no crop on account of his stupidity or laziness. In the same way God foresees our salvation or damnation as the result of our own free actions.

God also knows what could have happened in a given case, but actually did not happen. For example, He knows what would have been the mental development of James if James had studied at Columbia University instead of Harvard. Our Lord gives us an instance of this kind of knowledge. "Woe to thee, Corozain; woe to thee Bethsaida! For if in Tyre and Sidon had been wrought the miracles which have been wrought in you, they had long ago repented in sackcloth and ashes. But I say unto you, it shall be more tolerable for Tyre and Sidon in the day of judgment than for you" (Matt. 11,21-22). It is this special knowledge of God which makes it possible for Him to judge us with absolute justice on the Last Day. No one can complain of God's sentence, because the All-knowing Judge takes all possibilities into consideration.

2. God Is All-Wise.—He knows how to direct everything in the best manner in order to carry out His designs.

The Bible is full of examples of the wisdom of God, e.g., Joseph in Egypt, Moses, St. Paul. The whole creation is a revelation of the wisdom of God. Hence the Psalmist cries out: "How great are Thy works, O Lord; Thou hast made all things in wisdom" (Ps. 103-24).

C. Attributes of the Divine Will

1. God Is Almighty.—He can do all that He wills. To will and to do is one and the same thing with God. God cannot do what He cannot will. Hence He cannot do evil or contradict Himself. Nor can He give existence to a thing that contains a contradiction; for example, He cannot make a round triangle or a square circle.

The omnipotence of God is shown:

1. In the creation of the world. By one word of His almighty power God called heaven and earth into existence;

2. In the numerous miracles which He worked amongst men at all times.

Therefore the Angel Gabriel said to Mary: "No word shall be impossible with God" (Luke 1,37). And the Psalmist says: "Whatsoever the Lord pleased He hath done, in heaven, in earth, in the sea and in all the deeps" (Ps. 134,6).

2. God Is Holy.—He loves and wills only what is good and hates all evil.

"Holy, holy, holy, the Lord God of hosts" (Is. 6,3). Good in the proper and highest sense is God Himself; that is, His infinite perfection. God is therefore holy because He loves Himself. His holiness is the type of all holiness in creatures, who are holy if they love God above all things and all things for the sake of God. He says to us: "Be holy, because I am holy" (Lev. 11,44).

3. God Is Just.—He rewards all good and punishes all evil deeds.

We know from the Bible that God rewards good deeds and punishes evil deeds oftentimes even in this life; e.g., the Deluge, Sodom and Gomorrha, the High Priest Heli and his wicked sons. But perfect retribution will be made only in eternity: however, even in this life there is no true happiness for the wicked and no true unhappiness for the good. No wicked person is really happy, because his conscience will not give him any rest. No just man is really unhappy, because he possesses peace of heart and the well-grounded hope of eternal reward in Heaven.

God "will render to every man according to his works," "for there is no respect of persons with God" (Rom. 2,6,11).

4. God Is Good.—He loves all His creatures and loads them with benefits.

God loves all the creatures that He has made. "Not one of them is forgotten before God" (Luke 12,6). But God has an especial love for mankind. All that we are and all that we have, body and soul, all our powers of body and soul we owe to God. The greatest proof of His love is that He allowed His only Son to be put to death for the salvation of us sinners. Jesus said to Nicodemus: "God so loved the world as to give His only-begotten Son, that whosoever believeth in Him, may not perish, but may have life everlasting" (John 3,16).

5. God Is Merciful.—He willingly pardons all truly penitent sinners.

"As I live, saith the Lord God, I desire not the death of the wicked; but that the wicked turn from his way and live" (Ezech. 33,11).

6. God Is Long-suffering.—He often waits a long time before He punishes the sinner, in order to give him time for repentance and a change of life.

"The Lord dealeth patiently for your sake, not willing that any should perish, but that all should return to penance" (2 Pet. 3,9).

God is good to *all* His creatures, merciful to the *penitent* sinners, long-suffering with the *unrepentant sinners*.

7. God Is Truthful.—He can reveal nothing but truth, because He can neither deceive nor be deceived.

"God is not a man, that He should lie" (Num. 23,19). And St. Paul says: "It is impossible for God to lie" (Heb. 6,18).

God cannot be deceived, because He is omniscient; He cannot deceive, because He is All-holy.

8. God Is Faithful.—He surely keeps what He promises, and executes what He threatens.

"Heaven and earth shall pass away, but My word shall not pass away" (Mark 13,31).

SUGGESTIONS FOR STUDY AND REVIEW

1. What is God?
2. What names are given to God in the Old Testament?
3. Show in what the *nature* of God primarily consists.
4. How does our reason arrive at a notion of God and His perfections?
5. Read Longfellow's poem *The Monk Felix*. What lesson does it teach?
6. Explain the expressions, "God repents," "God is angry," "God hates the sinner."
7. Does the foreknowledge of God take away human liberty? Illustrate your answer by some examples.
8. Why can God pass an absolutely just sentence on all men at the Last Judgment?
9. Draw a lesson for your daily conduct from each attribute of God.
10. On what attributes of God do we base our Acts of Faith, Hope, Love and Contrition?
11. What attributes of God do the following parables illustrate: The Good Samaritan, The Lost Sheep, The Prodigal Son, The Rich Man and Lazarus, The Unmerciful Servant?
12. Find in the Gospels five examples of Christ's love and mercy for sinners.
13. *Reading:* Matt., chs. 5-7: *Sermon on the Mount.* What attributes of God are clearly revealed in the Sermon on the Mount? Quote chapter and verse.

CHAPTER II

The Blessed Trinity

"In the Name of the Father, and of the Son, and of the
Holy Ghost."—Matt. 28,19.

1. "Hear, O Israel, the Lord our God is *one* Lord" (Deut. 6,4).
These words of Moses sum up the religion of the Israelites. It
was their worship of the *one* God (monotheism) that distinguished the Israelites from the worshipers of *many* gods (polythe-
ism) by whom they were surrounded. For the Israelite there is
only *one Almighty Ruler* of the universe, only *one Supreme Wisdom* ordering all things, only *one Supreme Love* embracing all
things, only *one Divine Nature*, Essence or Substance.

2. The Trinity in the Old Testament.—Here and there in
the Old Testament a hint was thrown out that there were still
deeper depths to the mystery of God's nature. In Genesis (3,22)
God says: "Behold, Adam is become as one of *Us*," and in the
Book of Psalms (2,7): "Thou art My Son; this day have I begotten Thee." The "Spirit of God" is represented as "brooding over
the waters" at the dawn of creation. Divine Wisdom is personified
as "sitting by the throne of God" and as "coming out of the mouth
of the Most High, the First-born before all creatures" (Wis. 9,4;
Ecclus. 24,5). There are also mysterious references to the *Word*
of God. But to no Wise Man or Prophet was it given to probe
these mysterious allusions.

3. Christ Reveals the Mystery of the Trinity.—It was only
when the "fullness of time was come, and God sent His Son"
(Gal. 4,4) that the greatest Mystery of the Godhead was clearly
revealed—the *Mystery of the Most Blessed Trinity*—the mystery
that there are *three Persons* in the *one* God: the Father, the Son,
and the Holy Ghost (or Spirit).

a) The first revelation took place at the baptism of Christ:
"And Jesus being baptized forthwith came out of the water; and,
lo, the heavens were opened to Him; and He saw the *Spirit of
God* descending as a dove and coming upon Him. And behold a

voice from heaven, saying: This is *My beloved Son,* in Whom I am well pleased" (Matt. 3,16-17).

b) Before His ascension into Heaven, Christ said to His Apostles: "All power is given to Me in Heaven and in earth; going, therefore, teach ye all nations, baptizing them in the name of the Father, and of the Son, and of the Holy Ghost" (Matt. 28,18f.).

c) At the Last Supper Jesus said to His disciples: "I will ask the Father, and He shall give you another Paraclete, that He may abide with you forever, the Spirit of Truth" (John 14,16-17).

d) Of Himself Jesus said: "I and the Father are one" (John 10,30).

e) Of the Holy Ghost, St. Peter declared: "Ananias, why hath Satan tempted thy heart that thou shouldst lie to the Holy Ghost? . . . Thou hast not lied to men, but to *God*" (Acts 5,3-4).

Therefore each one of the three Persons is true God: the Father is true God, the Son is true God, the Holy Ghost is true God. But as there cannot be more than one true God, the three Divine Persons *must* be *one* God.

4. The Church Defends the Trinity against Heretics.—A number of heretics from the second to the fourth century denied the doctrine of the Blessed Trinity. Some said there were really no three Persons in God, but that the Father, the Son, and the Holy Ghost were only three *names* for one Person. *Arius* maintained that the Son was a creature of the Father, and not God from all eternity. He was unanimously condemned by the Council of Nicaea (325). *Macedonius* asserted that the Holy Ghost was a creature and the servant of the Son. This heresy was condemned by the Council of Constantinople (381).

The true doctrine of the Church is clearly set forth in the Creed published by the Councils of Nicaea and Constantinople, and more clearly still in the Athanasian Creed, which has been called the "war-song of faith."

5. The Athanasian Creed: "Whosoever desires to be saved, before all things it is necessary that he hold the Catholic faith. Which faith, except every one do keep entire and inviolate, without doubt he shall perish everlastingly. Now the Catholic faith is this:

"That we worship one God in Trinity, and Trinity in Unity, neither confounding the Persons nor dividing the substance.

THE BLESSED TRINITY

"For there is one Person of the Father, another of the Son, another of the Holy Ghost.

"But the Godhead of the Father, and of the Son, and of the Holy Ghost is *one*; the glory equal, the majesty co-eternal.

"As the Father is, such is the Son, such the Holy Ghost.

"The Father uncreated, the Son uncreated, the Holy Ghost uncreated.

"The Father infinite, the Son infinite, the Holy Ghost infinite.

"The Father eternal, the Son eternal, the Holy Ghost eternal.

"And yet there are not three eternal beings, but *one* Eternal; as also there are not three uncreated, nor three infinite beings, but *one* Uncreated, and *one* Infinite.

"In like manner the Father is Almighty, the Son Almighty, the Holy Ghost Almighty, and yet there are not three almighties, but *one* Almighty: So the Father is God; the Son God, the Holy Ghost God, and yet they are not three gods, but *one* God.

"So the Father is Lord, the Son is Lord, and the Holy Ghost is Lord. And yet they are not three lords, but *one* Lord. For as we are obliged by the Christian truth to acknowledge every Person singly to be God and Lord, so are we forbidden by the Catholic Religion to say there are three gods or three lords.

"The Father was made by no one, neither created nor begotten.

"The Son is by the Father alone, not made, nor created, but 'begotten.'

"The Holy Ghost is from the Father and the Son, not made, nor created, nor begotten, but 'proceeding.'

"So there is *one* Father, not three Fathers; *one* Son, not three Sons; *one* Holy Ghost, not three Holy Ghosts. And in this Trinity there is nothing before or after, nothing greater or less; but the whole three Persons are co-eternal together and co-equal.

"So that in all things, as was said above, the Unity is to be worshiped in Trinity, and the Trinity in Unity.

"He, therefore, that desires to be saved must thus believe of the Trinity."

6. All the actions of God towards creatures are common to the three Divine Persons. Still, we attribute the *works of omnipotence,* especially the creation, to the Father; the *works of wisdom,* and particularly the Redemption, to the Son; and the **works of love,** especially sanctification, to the Holy Spirit.

7. The Trinity, the Greatest of Mysteries.—The doctrine of the Most Blessed Trinity is a *Mystery,* in fact the greatest of all mysteries. It is impossible for our weak and limited intellect, which cannot even understand created things except imperfectly, to understand a mystery which is infinitely above all created things.

Whilst St. Augustine was preparing himself to explain the mystery of the Blessed Trinity to his people, it seemed to him that he was walking by the shore of a vast ocean, contemplating its mysterious and unfathomable depth. Suddenly he saw before him a little boy, amusing himself by boring a hole in the sand, and pouring into it from a shell the water of the ocean. The Saint asked him what he was doing. "I am trying," the child replied, "to empty the sea into this hole."—"Then you are trying to do an impossible thing."—"Not more impossible," answered the child, "than for you to understand or explain the mystery of the Blessed Trinity." And with these words the little boy disappeared.

8. The Trinity and Human Reason.—Though no created intelligence can understand the Trinity, we can nevertheless refute the objections brought against it, and illustrate the mystery itself by comparisons taken from nature and from the human soul.

The *objections* against the Trinity arise from a false notion of the doctrine itself. The Church does not teach that $1 = 3$; that would be the case if she taught that there was *one* God and at the same time that there were *three* gods, or *one* Person and at the same time *three* Persons in God. What she does teach is, that there is *one* God *in* three Persons. The Unity refers to the nature, the Trinity to the Persons.

Holy Scripture calls the Son the "brightness of the glory," the figure of the substance of the Father (Heb. 1,3) and the "Word" of the Father (John 1,1) ; the Holy Ghost the "Charity of God" (Rom. 5,5). With the aid of these expressions St. Anselm (d.1109) endeavored to bring the mystery of the Blessed Trinity a little nearer home to us. A spiritual being, he says, can make itself the object of its thought. It sees itself as in a "mirror." With God the *Father* this knowledge of Himself is a necessary and eternal Thought which is the most perfect expression of His Being. The Father expresses this Thought in an eternal Word, and this Word is the *Son* : "In the beginning was the Word, and the Word was with God." The Word is called a Son because generated, brought forth, not physically, but spiritually as our own mind gives birth to such thoughts as temperance, justice, longitude, latitude. Father and Son know each other as the most perfect Good and hence have for each other an eternal *Love*. This Love between the Father and the Son is the *Holy Spirit*.

The various comparisons used to illustrate the mystery of the Blessed Trinity are well summed up by Father Sheen as follows: "Just as water, ice and steam are all manifestations of the same substance; just as the length, breadth and thickness of a cathedral do not make three cathedrals, but one; just as carbon, diamond and graphite are manifestations of one and the same nature; just as the color, perfume and form of a rose do not make three roses, but one; just as the soul, the intellect and the will do not make three lives, but one; just as $1 \times 1 \times 1 = 1$ and not 3, so in a much more mysterious way there are three Persons in the Blessed Trinity and yet only one God."

9. Importance of the Trinity.—The Mystery of the Trinity is the *principal* and *fundamental* doctrine of Christianity; to reject it would be to deny the Christian Faith. The Incarnation, which is the source of all grace and blessing to us, is inconceivable without the Trinity. In the name of the Blessed Trinity the Church administers all the Sacraments; in the name of the Blessed Trinity she consecrates and blesses persons, places and things; in the name of the Blessed Trinity she begins and ends all her prayers. In the name of the Blessed Trinity we were received into the Church by Baptism. As often as we make the sign of the cross or repeat the *Gloria Patri* we profess our faith in this mystery. When our last hour draws near, the priest accompanies our departing soul with the words: "Though she has sinned, yet she did not deny the Father, Son, and Holy Ghost." In the name of the Blessed Trinity our mortal remains are consigned to their last resting place.

SUGGESTIONS FOR STUDY AND REVIEW

1. When is the Feast of the Most Blessed Trinity celebrated? Read the Proper of the Mass for this Feast. What does it tell us about the Blessed Trinity? (Read the *Introit,* the *Collect,* the *Epistle, Gradual, Gospel, Offertory, Secret, Preface, Communion* and *Postcommunion.*)
2. Prepare a brief paper on the Blessed Trinity, using the following outline: (*a*) Revelation of the Trinity in the Old Testament; (*b*) in the New Testament. (*c*) The Blessed Trinity in the teaching of the Church. (*d*) The Blessed Trinity and Reason. (*e*) The importance of the Mystery of the Trinity.
3. Copy the following texts: John 3,5; 1 Cor. 3,16; John 15,26; Luke 1,35; John 14,16 and 26; 20,22; 2 Pet. 1,21; Acts 20,28. What do these texts tell us about the Holy Ghost?
4. State whether the following propositions are true or false:

   a) "A father must exist before a son; therefore the Divine Father must have existed before the Divine Son."
   b) "Each of the Divine Persons possesses His *own* Divine Nature."
   c) "The Holy Ghost proceeds from the Father and the Son."
5. What was St. Patrick's illustration of the Blessed Trinity?

CHAPTER III

The Creation of the World

"In the beginning God created heaven and earth."—GEN. 1,1.

1. God, the Creator of Heaven and Earth.—God created, i.e., made out of nothing by an act of His will, the heavens and the earth, and all that is in them. "In the beginning God created heaven and earth" (Gen. 1,1). The mother of the Machabees said to her youngest son: "I beseech thee, my son, look upon heaven and earth, and all that is in them, and consider that *God made them out of nothing*, and mankind also" (2 Mach. 7,28).

2. The World Not Eternal.—The world did not exist from eternity, but was created in time, or rather at the beginning of time. Before the creation of the world there was no time. On the eve of His Passion Jesus prayed: "And now glorify Thou Me, O Father, with Thyself, with the glory which I had, *before the world was*, with Thee" (John 17,5). From these words it is evident that the world is not eternal.

3. God Created the World of His Own Free Choice.—God is infinitely rich and happy in Himself. He needs nothing besides Himself. He created other beings because He is infinitely good and desired to impart His goodness to them. "Because God is good, we exist," says St. Augustine.

4. God Created the World for His Own Glory.—The highest purpose of all created things is the glory of God. The glory of God consists in the revelation of His perfections to His rational creatures. By acknowledging these perfections through acts of adoration, love and thanks, men and Angels give glory to God. He wished "to show them the greatness of His works, that they might praise the name which He hath sanctified and glory in His wondrous acts" (Ecclus. 17,7-8). By giving glory to God, they lay the foundation of their own happiness; if they fail to do this, God is glorified by the exercise of His justice towards them. Hence God always attains the *first purpose* of creation—His own glory; the *second purpose* of creation—the *happiness of His rational creatures*—He attains only if they co-operate with Him.

5. God Created the World Good.—The arrangement and purpose of the world are good. God did not will evil of any kind, nor could He will it. Evil is the result of the abuse of free will given by God to men and Angels. "God saw all the things that He had made, and they were very good" (Gen. 1,31).

6. The Work of the Six Days.—Did God create the world in 6x24 hours? Some hold this view, while others with very good reasons reject it. If we look at the seventh day or day of rest, we find that it continued uninterruptedly to the present time. That means a duration of thousands of years. Hence, we conclude that the six previous days are also to be taken as six indefinitely long periods of time. That this is really the case is further proved by the existence of fossils of plants and animals in the interior of the earth and of the stalactites and stalagmites in the Mammoth Cave, Kentucky, and in similar caves in various parts of the world. It took thousands of years for these columns and cones of carbonate of lime to form, and many thousands of years for the production of coal in strata in the earth by the decomposition of vegetable matter.

Must we assume that God created the light, the firmament, the air, the water, the plants, etc., in the order in which they are recorded in the first chapter of Genesis? Not at all. The most natural explanation seems to be this: The sacred writer, being obliged to follow some order in his description, arranges the work of creation as follows: Three days are devoted to the creation of the *habitats* (abodes) and three to the creation of the *inhabitants*. The light was created first as a general preparation; then the firmament for the stars, and finally the air, the water, the earth with its vegetation for the winged animals, the aquatic animals, the land animals, and man.

7. The Work of Creation and the Week of Seven Days.—No human being witnessed the creation. Of themselves men did not conceive the idea of the creation of the world through *one* God. This was *revealed* to them. In all probability God revealed the fact of creation to Adam, the first man. *How* He did this, we do not know. Of the many guesses hazarded by various scholars, the following seems to have most in its favor. God, as we know from the Bible, makes His revelations known to men in two ways: sometimes through an Angel in human form, as in the case of the Annunciation; at other times by means of a vision granted to a human being in a dream or in an ecstasy, as in the case of St. Joseph and of St. Peter. If we suppose that God used the latter method, then the six days of creation would be six successive visions, each divided from the other by a period of darkness. God chose *six* days because He wished to inculcate the keeping holy of the seventh day as a day of rest. The "deep sleep" which God cast upon Adam, when He created Eve from one of Adam's ribs, may also be regarded as an ecstasy or a vision of Adam.

8. Science and the Biblical Account of Creation.—Since the Bible is not a natural science book, it is the task of physical science to investigate the physical history of the world. But without falling back upon the Almighty Creator of heaven and earth, the natural scientist cannot answer such questions as the following: (1) Where does primary matter come from? (2) What is the cause of motion in matter? (3) What is the origin of Life in plants, animals and men? (4) What is the cause of order and design in nature?

SUGGESTIONS FOR STUDY AND REVIEW

1. When a sculptor makes a statue of Washington out of a block of marble, can he be said to have *created* a statue of Washington? If the same sculptor said to a block of marble: Let a statue of Washington be made, and if the block of marble turned into a likeness of Washington, would that be creation?
2. Geologists tell us that the earth is more than a hundred thousand years old, and astronomers tell us that it has taken the light of some stars millions of years to reach the earth. Do these statements contradict the account of creation given in Genesis?
3. In order to answer some of the stock charges brought against the Biblical account of the creation, remember, above all, the *purpose* of the inspired writer. Moses wished to teach that God is the Creator, that all things are the work of His hand; that God created without effort, by a mere act of His will. To make this clear to his people, he must be *concrete*. He cannot use scientific terms. So he takes the example of a vast house in course of construction. "At first God lays down the site—a cavernous void. He creates light and flashes it into the empty space. He rears the dwellings for His servants. He unrolls the firmament for His suns. He builds airy cages for His birds. He sluices down water into the hollows of the earth for His fishes. He fans the earth dry for His plants and trees, His beasts and men. The buildings have arisen, but they are still tenantless. And now, on the fourth day, come the stars to fleck the firmament. On the fifth day appear the fishes and birds to people sea and air. On the sixth day come the animals to claim the dry land. And finally comes man, the crown and lord of creation, to shepherd and name his flock. On the seventh day God rests—not that He is tired, but to teach man the important lesson that the seventh day is the Day of the Lord" (Paffrath-Kean, *Stock Charges Against the Bible,* St. Louis: B. Herder Book Co., p.34).
4. What do the following texts teach about the Creation: John 1,3; Acts 4,24; Rom. 11,36?

CHAPTER IV

Divine Providence

"He made the little and the great, and He hath equally care of all."—Wıs. 6,8.

1. God Preserves and Governs the World.—The whole world which God created would return to its original nothingness if He were to withdraw from it His supporting power for a single instant. "How could anything endure if Thou wouldst not?" (Wis. 11,26). By the same power of His will with which He created the world, He causes it also to continue, in the manner He pleases, and as long as He pleases. "God upholds all things by the word of His power" (Heb. 1,3).

He takes care of all things, orders all things, and in His wisdom and goodness directs all things to the end for which He created the world.

2. Divine Providence.—This government and direction of the world by God is called *Divine Providence* (Lat. *pro*, forward, and *video*, I see).

The *Providence* of God extends even to the smallest things. "God made the little and the great, and He hath equally care of all" (Wis. 6,8). "Are not two sparrows sold for a farthing? And not one of them shall fall to the ground without your Father. But the very hairs of your head are all numbered. Fear not, therefore; better are you than many sparrows" (Matt. 10,29-31).

In preserving and governing the world, God as a rule makes use of the *laws of nature*; still, He is always the Lord of nature. Whenever His wise designs demand it, He can change the nature of created things, increase or diminish their forces, substitute for these forces His own divine power—in a word, perform *miracles*.

God's Providence directs the course of the history of the world. We see His guiding hand especially in the history of the Israelites, in the preparation of the world for the coming of Christ, in the destruction of Jerusalem, in the dispersion and preservation of the Jewish race, but most of all in the history of the Catholic Church.

3. Divine Providence and the Problem of Evil.—Those who deny the Providence of God say: (1) If a *holy* God governed the world, He would not permit evil. (2) If a *good* God governed the world, there would be no suffering. (3) If a *just* God governed the world, the wicked would never prosper, nor would evil ever befall the good. We answer:

1. God does not will *moral evil* (sin), but He permits it, because He has created man free, and because He knows also how to turn evil into good. Joseph said to his brothers: "You thought evil against me, but God turned it into good" (Gen. 50,20). *God turned even the murder of Our Savior by the Jews to the salvation of the World.* By creating His rational creatures with free will, God wished to confer a benefit on them, not to bring sin into the world. He has given everyone sufficient grace to make good use of his freedom.

2. *Suffering and afflictions* (physical evils) are either caused by the forces of nature, such as earthquakes, cyclones, etc., or by the fault of man through the abuse of his free will, such as murders, wars, etc., or are sent by God to punish man, such as the Deluge.

3. *God permits or inflicts sufferings* because they are not evils in the strict sense of the word, but may be the means of acquiring the greatest good, that is, eternal happiness. There are so many sufferings in the world in order that the sinner may acknowledge the chastisement of God and mend his ways and not perish forever; and in order that the just may be more and more purified and gain more abundant merits and thus obtain a higher reward in Heaven. "We deserve to suffer these things," said the brothers of Joseph, "because we have sinned against our brother" (Gen. 42,21). "Gold and silver are tried in the fire, but acceptable men in the furnace of humiliation" (Ecclus. 2,5). If there were no sufferings in the world, men would soon forget that "we have not here a lasting city, but we seek one that is to come" (Heb. 13,14).

4. God often permits the wicked to prosper, whilst evil befalls the good:

a) Because He does not only wish to deter the sinner from his evil ways by punishment, but also wishes to win him back by benefits;

b) Because He reserves to Himself the right to punish the wicked and to reward the good, especially in eternity;

c) Because He wishes to punish the good in this life for the few or smaller sins they may have committed, and to reward the wicked for the little good which they do. Abraham says to the rich man buried in hell: "Son, remember that thou didst receive good things in thy lifetime, and likewise Lazarus evil things; but now he is comforted, and thou art tormented" (Luke 16,25).

4. Christian Optimism.—We ought to receive the sufferings that come upon us as graces of God, as proofs of the divine mercy and love, for "Whom the Lord loveth, He chastiseth" (Heb. 12,6), and at the same time we should make use of them as a means of showing our love for God and of becoming daily more like our suffering Savior. "Dearly beloved," says Peter, "if you partake of the sufferings of Christ, rejoice that, when His glory shall be revealed, you may also be glad with exceeding joy" (I Pet. 4,13). *Optimism*, not *Pessimism*, is the true Christian attitude. "To them that love God," says St. Paul, "*all things* work together unto good" (Rom. 8,28).

SUGGESTIONS FOR STUDY AND REVIEW

1. Prepare a short paper, to be read or delivered before the class, on "Divine Providence." You may use the following questions for your outline:
   a) How does God preserve and govern the world?
   b) What do we call the supreme care of God in preserving and governing the world? Explain the word *Providence*.
   c) If God takes care of all things, why are we subject to moral and physical evils, to sin and suffering?
   d) What should be our attitude in the face of sufferings and afflictions?
2. Copy the following texts and use them in answering the above questions: Matt. 5,11-12; Luke 6,24; I Pet. 5,7; Matt. 6,26-33
3. *Reading:*
   a) *Imitation of Christ*, Bk. I, ch. xii, and Bk. II, ch. xi.
   b) Zimmerman—Zybura, *The Problem of Evil and Human Destiny:* Introduction by Bishop Schrembs.

CHAPTER V

The Spirit World

"He hath given His Angels charge over thee, to keep thee in all thy ways."—Ps. 90,11.

1. The Invisible Creation.—Besides the visible world God also created an invisible one, the innumerable spirits whom we call *Angels*. We call them Angels, that is, "messengers," because God makes use of them to reveal His will to men and to carry out His decrees. "Are the Angels not *ministering spirits*," says St. Paul, "sent to minister for them who shall receive the inheritance of salvation?" (Heb. 1,14).

2. Scripture and the Spirit World.—The existence of spiritual beings endowed with understanding and free will is proved from the Bible. In the Old Testament we find Angels guarding the entrance to the Garden of Eden; Angels ascending and descending the ladder which Jacob saw in his dream; and an Angel accompanying the young Tobias on his journey. In the New Testament Angels announce the birth of the Savior and of His precursor; Angels minister to Our Lord after His temptation; an Angel comforts Him in His Agony; and Angels console the Apostles after Christ's Ascension.

Since the end of the fourth century the Angels are represented in Christian art with *wings* to symbolize their spiritual nature. This symbolism is also used in Scripture. The Cherubim on the Ark of the Covenant had two wings, the Seraphim in Isaias (6,2) six.

3. The Spirit World and Human Reason.—Our unaided reason can neither prove nor disprove the existence of pure spirits; but it can show the fittingness of their existence. The visible creation presents the spectacle of a great pyramid. At the base we find *inorganic nature*, chemicals and minerals, the lowest form of being. These are succeeded by three *grades of living things*: plants, irrational animals, and man. In his soul man resembles God; in his body, the irrational animals. He is partly corporeal and partly spiritual. To make the scale of created beings complete, all that is required is a being that is purely spiritual; an Angel is such a

85

being, and it is quite fitting that God should include the Angels in His plan of creation.

4. The Number and Dignity of the Angels.—Jesus speaks of legions of Angels, St. Paul of many thousands, and the Prophet Daniel says, speaking of God: "Thousands of thousands ministered to Him, and ten thousand times a hundred thousand stood before Him" (7,10).

On account of their spiritual nature the Angels are superior to man in knowledge and power. They were also endowed from the beginning with sanctifying grace in order that they might be able to merit the supernatural happiness for which they were destined by God. As they were beings with free will, it was fitting that they should be *subjected to a trial* before being admitted to the vision of God.

Holy Scripture distinguishes several classes of Angels. Theologians divide the Angels into three *hierarchies,* each of which contains three orders, or *choirs:*

Angels, Archangels, Virtues;
Powers, Principalities, Dominations;
Thrones, Cherubim, Seraphim.

Only three Angels are mentioned in Scripture by name: *Michael*—"Who is like God?", *Gabriel*—"Man of God," and *Raphael*—"God heals."

5. Good and Bad Angels.—The Angels that were found faithful in their trial obtained supernatural happiness; they were permitted to see God face to face. Many of the Angels, however, rebelled against God and were cast from Him forever and hurled into hell. "God spared not the Angels that sinned, but delivered them . . . to the lower Hell, unto torments, to be reserved unto judgment" (2 Pet. 2,4).

Pride was the cause of the fall of the Angels. They wished to be like God; that is, independent of Him. "Pride is the beginning of all sin" (Ecclus. 10,15).

The leader of the fallen angels is called in Scripture the *devil* (*diabolus,* calumniator, liar) and *Satan,* the Hebrew word for "enemy." Later on, he was also called *Lucifer* (Morning Star) from the words of Isaias about the proud king of Babylon: "How art thou fallen from heaven, O Lucifer. . . . Thou saidst in thy heart: I will ascend into Heaven, . . . and I will be like the Most High" (Is. 14,12ff.). The Jews at the time of Christ identified him with *Beelzebub,* the chief god of the Philistines: "This man [Jesus] casteth not out devils but by Beelzebub, the prince of devils" (Matt. 12,24). St. Paul calls all the gods of the pagans *demons* (1 Cor. 10,20).

I have felt thee in my thoughts, fighting with sin for me.

St. Michael Expelling Lucifer from Heaven

6. The Good Angels Love Us.—The Good Angels love us because they love God. They protect us in soul and body, pray for us and exhort us to do good. St. Paul calls them "ministering spirits sent to minister for them who shall receive the inheritance of salvation" (Heb. 1,14). "When thou didst pray with tears, . . . I offered thy prayer to the Lord," the Angel Raphael said to Tobias (12,12).

That everyone has a *Guardian Angel*, has never been defined by the Church, but has always been accepted as true. Our belief is based on the words of Christ: "See that you despise not one of these little ones, for . . . *their Angels* in Heaven always see the face of My Father who is in Heaven" (Matt. 18,10). When St. Peter, after his deliverance from prison, knocked at the door of the house where the Christians were assembled, his friends would not believe that it was he, but said: "It is his Angel" (Acts 12,15).

"How great is the dignity of the soul," writes St. Jerome; "each one has from its birth an Angel for its special protection." And St. Basil the Great says: "No one can deny that every Christian has an Angel at his side who teaches and directs him."

7. The Wicked Angels Hate Us and Envy Us.—The wicked Angels hate us because they hate God. They try to injure us in soul and body and, by enticing us to sin, to plunge us into eternal misery. "Your adversary the devil, as a roaring lion, goeth about seeking whom he may devour" (1 Pet. 5,8). The fall of our first parents, the treason of Judas and the lie told by Ananias are attributed in Scripture to the wiles of the devil. The devil even tempted Our Lord (Matt 4,1ff.).

The devil cannot force us to commit sin. By watchfulness and prayer we can resist all his wiles. "Resist the devil, and he will fly from you," says St. James (4,7). Since the death of Christ, the Fathers of the Church tell us, the devil is like a chained dog. If we go out of his way, we need not fear him; he barks, but cannot bite.

From the history of Job, we know that the devils have power to afflict men in various ways, to destroy their property and to bring disease upon them. They can even take *possession* of the whole man, without, however, being able to do violence to his will. God permits this, because He knows how to make the snares of the evil spirits serve unto His own honor and the salvation of souls. The Church makes use of *Exorcisms* as a protection against the harmful influences of the devil.

The power of Satan will manifest itself once more before the end of the world during the reign of the so-called *Antichrist,* who is mentioned by St. John in his first Epistle (2,28) and by St. Paul (2 Thess. 2,3ff.).

False notions about the wicked spirits are often ascribed to the Church. They are based on false interpretations of pictures, on legends, humorous stories, folk tales, and superstition (e.g., *witchcraft*). All these things have nothing to do with the teachings of the Church.

SUGGESTIONS FOR STUDY AND REVIEW

1. Summarize the chapter on the Spirit World in a brief essay of not more than 250 words.
2. Look up the following texts and note what they tell you about the good and wicked angels: Acts 8,6-7; John 13,2; Acts 5,3; Matt. 4,24; 26,41; Mark 16,17; Luke 15,10; 10,18; 2 Cor. 11,14; Apoc. 8,2-4.
3. How are the Archangels Michael, Gabriel and Raphael represented in Christian art? When are their feasts celebrated? When is the feast of the Holy Guardian Angels kept? Do you know a hymn to the Guardian Angels?
4. Read the *Offertory of the Mass for the Dead.* What does it tell you about St. Michael?
5. *Readings:*
    a) Epistle for the 21st Sunday after Pentecost (Eph. 6,10-17);
    b) Exorcisms at Baptism, at the Blessing of Holy Water, and of Baptismal Water on Holy Saturday.

St. Frances of Rome and Her Guardian Angel

St. Frances (1384-1440) was often permitted to see her Guardian Angel, and to him she had recourse in all her trials and temptations. If she fell into any fault, a sadness overspread his countenance; but as soon as she repented, he reappeared full of joy and gladness.

"Who Made the Devil?"

"Who created the Angels?" the pastor asked the children in the catechism class. The answer was easy: God. "But who made the devil?" There was the difficulty! They thought, and thought again. Suddenly one exclaimed: "God created him an Angel, and he made himself a devil."

CHAPTER VI

Origin of the Human Race

"God, who made the world and all things therein, . . . hath made of one all mankind, to dwell upon the whole face of the earth."—Acts 17,24 and 26.

1. Man, the Crown and Lord of the Visible Creation.—When God had "formed out of the ground all the beasts of the earth and all the fowls of the air," He crowned His work by creating *Man* and placing him at the head of the visible world. "God said: Let Us make man to Our image and likeness; and let him have dominion over the fishes of the sea, and the fowls of the air, and the beasts, and the whole earth. . . . And the Lord God formed man of the slime of the earth and breathed into his face the breath of life, and man became a living soul. . . . Then God took one of Adam's ribs and formed it into a woman; . . . Adam called her Eve, because she was the mother of all the living" (Gen. 1,26; 2,7; 2,22; 3,20).

This narrative clearly shows:
1. That man is the crown and lord of the visible world;
2. That he consists of soul and body;
3. That in his body he resembles the other living creatures, but in his soul he is related to God;
4. That all men are descended from one man and woman, from Adam and Eve;
5. That woman was to be the companion of man, not his slave.
The Church has made no definite declaration concerning the creation of the human body. St. Augustine maintained that a purely literal interpretation of the Biblical account is unworthy of God. When He made the first man, God did not go about it as children do when they build a snowman or fashion dolls of clay. Here, too, as in the creation of light, God's almighty *fiat*, "let it be made," sufficed.

The creation of man is described as a twofold operation: the forming of man's body out of the slime of the earth, and the infusion of the soul into the body. Hence the question of the origin of man is also a twofold one: the origin of his body, and the origin of his soul.

2. Origin of the Human Body.—Extreme evolutionists tell us that man was a new species sprung from some lower animal stock. They assume as their starting point one living cell. Out of this cell, they claim, all the myriad forms of plants, animals and men have gradually evolved (developed). This conjecture—for it is no more—does not do away with the Creator. The Creator is necessary to make possible the existence of the first living cell and of the germs required for such manifold developments. An examination of the very word "evolution," or development, makes this clear. Evolution means the act of unfolding or developing. Now, there was either something in the first cell that could be "unfolded" and grow, or there was nothing there, and in this case evolution is impossible; for it remains eternally true that *ex nihilo nihil fit,* "from nothing comes nothing." You cannot develop a film, if there is nothing on the film to be developed or brought out.

Thus we see that the evolutionary theory does not exclude the Creator. Hence, if we assume that the evolution of created living cells took place under the directing hand of God, there is no objection against such an assumption. The Church has left the question open. Up to the present, however, no proofs have been forthcoming for such wholesale evolution. Scientists have made it seem more or less probable that evolution has taken place within the lower forms of animal life, such as mollusks and insects. It seems that new species of insects have been developed out of earlier ones. But not a shred of evidence has been produced to prove that higher orders of living beings have been evolved from lower ones. The evolution of all the forms of life which we see in the world today, and therefore also of the human body, from one original cell, may be *possible in theory,* but it is *actually highly improbable.*

"Some theologians hold that the Bible does not preclude the theory of the descent of man from the beast. Yet this theory cannot be accepted save with certain reservations. It must be maintained that, in the final analysis, God really did form the body of man from the dust of the earth. He might have caused a species of animal gradually to develop into a more perfect species, until it was fitted to receive a rational, immortal soul. And then, into this body, formed by long evolution from the dust of the earth, He may have breathed a human soul; and when He did so, He created man or Adam."

—PAFFRATH-KEAN, *Stock Charges Against the Bible,* p. 41.

3. Origin of the Human Soul.—The words: "God breathed into his face the breath of life, and man became a living soul," show that the soul of man is not formed out of any kind of matter, but created directly by God as a spiritual substance and united with the body. Science has not proved, nor can it ever prove, that the spiritual, the intellectual part of man is derived from animal ancestors. A brief consideration of the difference between man and the highest brute, the anthropoid (man-like) ape, will clearly demonstrate that man and beast belong to two totally different orders of being:

1. Man has the gift of speech and learns languages; the ape has not this gift.
2. Man has the power of forming abstract ideas or thoughts; the ape has no such power.
3. Man is capable of the highest culture and progress; he inquires into the past and the future, into the powers of nature, into science, art, religion. The ape, like all other lower animals, never shows the faintest sign of progress; he has only one concern: to preserve his life and to propagate his species.
4. Man is free. He deliberates and chooses. He is self-conscious. The ape acts only by instinct.

Origen, the great Biblical scholar of the early Church, taught that God created the souls of all men when He created the world. This doctrine of the so-called "pre-existence of souls" is condemned by the Church.

4. The Soul of Man Is Spiritual and Immortal.—The human soul is spiritual; that is, not composed of matter even in the most refined form. We know that it is spiritual because it produces spiritual effects by its two faculties, the *intellect* and the *will.* Being spiritual, the soul can exist without the body. It cannot die. God alone who gave it its spiritual nature could destroy it. "The dust [i.e., the body] returns to its earth from whence it was, and the spirit returns to God Who gave it" (Eccles. 12,7). "Fear not them that kill the body," says Our Lord, "and are not able to kill the soul" (Matt. 10,28). To the Good Thief on the cross, He said: "This day thou shalt be with Me in paradise" (Luke 23,43). He teaches the same truth in the parable of the Rich Man and Lazarus (Luke 16). The Fifth Lateran Council (1512) condemned "all who assert that the rational soul is mortal, or that there is only one soul in all mankind."

5. All Men Are Descended from One Pair.—In his discourse to the Athenians, St. Paul declared: "God made of one all mankind to dwell upon the whole face of the earth" (Acts 17,26). The doctrine of the unity of the human race is an article of our holy Faith.

But, it may be objected, are not whites, Negroes, Hottentots,

Chinese, and American Indians so different from one another that they must belong to different species of men?

Science has long ago answered this objection. The comparative study of languages has proved that all languages are related; and it is an historical fact that Asia is the original home of the various races of mankind. In 1889 the famous scientist Virchow said: "We must admit the possibility that all races and tribes descended from *one* human pair."

All men have the same moral and religious disposition; all speak an articulated language; all are capable of spiritual and mental development. There are differences of color, of shape of the skull, of the hair, etc., between the various races; but there are also so many points of resemblance that it is impossible to fix the exact number of races.

6. The Age of the Human Race.—According to the Hebrew text of the Bible there were about 4166 years between the creation of Adam and the birth of Christ; according to the Samaritan text, about 4466 years; and according to the Septuagint, 5513 years. Which text is the correct one? There is no means of finding out. There may be wide gaps in the lists of the Patriarchs, and then several thousand years more would have to be added. Hence, we are not tied down, in our interpretation of Scripture, to any definite number of years for the age of man.

Profane history cannot throw any more light on the age of the human race than the existing texts of the Bible. It seems certain that about the year 4000 B.C. the peoples dwelling in the valley of the Euphrates and the Tigris had developed a high degree of civilization. The history of Egypt can be traced back several hundred years more, to about the year 4200, when we find the first traces of the division of the year into 365 days.

Prehistoric science has nothing but guesses to offer in answer to our question. These guesses run from 1,000,000 to 25,000 years, which makes it clear that data are wanting for forming even an approximate estimate of the antiquity of man.*

SUGGESTIONS FOR STUDY AND REVIEW

1. In what does the greatness and littleness of man consist? You can answer this question by carefully reading the Biblical account of the creation of man.
2. Is the theory that the *body* of man was evolved from some lower animal condemned by the Church?

---

*The case is still very much the same today. Currently, scientists are estimating that the age of the human race is approximately 25,000 to 150,000 years. —*Editor,* 1990.

3. What must we hold in regard to the origin of the *soul* of man?
4. Show that the soul of man is spiritual and immortal.
5. Show the essential differences between man and the highest of the lower animals.
6. What do we know about the age of the human race from the Bible? from profane history? from the prehistoric sciences?
7. Answer the objections brought against the descent of the human race from one pair.
8. Summarize this chapter in an essay of not more than 250 words.
9. *Reading:* Paffrath-Kean, *Stock Charges Against the Bible,* pp. 37-45.

CHAPTER VII

Elevation and Fall of Man

"God created man incorruptible, . . . but by the envy of the devil death came into the world."—WIS. 2,23.

I. ELEVATION OF MAN

1. Man, an Image of God.—"And God said: Let Us make man to Our image and likeness" (Gen. 2,18). Man's likeness to God is to be found in his soul. The following parallel will show in what respects the human soul resembles God, and in what respects it differs from Him:

God is eternal, unchangeable, triune, a pure Spirit; the *human soul* is created, immortal, changeable, a spirit but united to a body.

God is omniscient and all-wise in His intelligence; the *human soul* has intelligence, but its knowledge is limited, as is also its wisdom, prudence, and discretion.

God's will is all-holy, all-just, infinitely good, merciful, truthful, faithful; *man's will* is made holy by grace, and is disposed to justice, goodness, mercy, truthfulness, fidelity.

In His operations God is almighty: He creates by a simple act of His will; *the operations of man* are limited; he cannot create, but he can give new forms to existing things.

2. The Supernatural Image of God in Man.—The first man was not only the *natural image* of God, resembling God in his soul; the bountiful Creator also wished His rational creature to come as near to resembling Him as it is possible for a creature to come. He destined him for a *supernatural end*, the eternal vision of God and communion with God in Heaven. And in order to enable him to attain this end by his own activity, God raised him above all earthly, temporal things by endowing him with *sanctifying grace*. Adam was thus not only *good*, as all the things that God had created were good; he was *holy* and in a very special manner pleasing to God. And because he was holy, God *adopted him as His child* and gave him the right to inherit the Kingdom of Heaven. This holiness of our first parent with its accompanying rights and privileges is called the *supernatural image of God in* *man.* "Adam was created," says the Council of Trent, "in justice and holiness; he was a *partaker of the divine nature.*"

3. Special Privileges of Our First Parents.—Together with sanctifying grace a number of extraordinary privileges were granted to our first parents:

a) They possessed a higher knowledge than we do. "God filled them with the knowledge of understanding and created in them the science of the spirit" (Ecclus. 17,5f.). Adam gave proof of his insight into the inner nature of things by giving appropriate names to all the animals (Gen. 2,20). He was also enlightened by God in regard to his supernatural destiny.

b) Their senses never rebelled against reason, the flesh against the spirit. "They were both naked . . . and were not ashamed" (Gen. 2,25). "Just as their souls obeyed God," says St. Augustine, "so their body obeyed the soul and was subject to it without resistance."

c) They were never to be subjected to disease, suffering or death. "God created man incorruptible" (Wis. 2,23). The immortality of their body was dependent on the *tree of life,* whose fruits were a protection against sickness and death. Their bodies were not immortal in the same sense as their souls. Their souls were *absolutely* immortal; it was impossible for them to die. Immortality belongs to the very nature of the soul; whereas the body is by nature subject to death.

d) They were placed in a lovely garden, the Garden of Eden, or Paradise, where "all manner of trees grew, fair to behold and pleasant to eat of."

4. "A Little Less than the Angels."—The happiness of our first parents in the Garden of Eden was almost equal to the happiness of the Angels when they were created. They enjoyed the peace of innocence and the possession of God. God Himself conversed with them. Legends of the perfect bliss of primitive man are preserved among heathen nations. This age of the world was called the *Golden Age.* The Greek poet Hesiod says that "men lived then like gods."

2. THE FALL OF MAN

Adam received Sanctifying Grace with the special privileges accompanying it not only for himself, but also for all his descendants. According to God's dispensation his supernatural as well as his natural gifts were to descend to the whole human race—but on one condition, viz., that he should remain faithful and obedient to God, his Creator.

1. The Trial.—Like the Angels, our first parents were subjected to a trial. "And the Lord God took man and put him into the Paradise of pleasure, to dress it and keep it. And He *commanded* him, saying, 'Of every tree of Paradise thou shalt eat, but of the tree of knowledge of good and evil thou shalt not eat. For in what day soever thou shalt eat of it, thou shalt die the death' " (Gen. 2,15-17).

THE FIRST SIN AND ITS PUNISHMENT
"And He cast out Adam: and placed before the paradise of pleasure Cherubims and a flaming sword." (Gen. 3,24.)

2. The Fall.—Seduced by the devil in the shape of a serpent, our first parents transgressed the divine command. "Eve took of the fruit and did eat and gave to her husband, who did eat" (Gen. 3,5). The sin of our first parents was

1. *A Manifold Sin:* a sin of *pride*—they wished to be like God; a sin of *unbelief*—they believed the devil more than God; a sin of *disobedience*—they did what God had expressly forbidden them to do; a sin of *ingratitude*—God had bestowed the greatest possible favors upon them.

2. A Grievous Sin.—God had given them only one command, which they could have easily obeyed; God had threatened them with the severest punishments if they transgressed His command: from the severity of the penalty they could readily see the importance of the command; they possessed a higher knowledge and were well aware that their sin would bring the greatest misfortunes upon themselves and their descendants.

The tradition of the Fall is preserved in many ancient myths. Well known is the story of *Pandora.* Jupiter gave Pandora a box inclosing all human ills, which escaped over the earth when the box was opened by her out of curiosity; *Hope,* which was also in the box, was all that she prevented from escaping. According to the *Avesta,* the sacred book of the ancient Persians, the serpent was created by the wicked god Ahriman and afterwards seduced the first man to commit sin. Among the Pygmies of the Andaman Islands the story is told that the highest God, *Puluga,* forbade men to gather the the first and best fruits of each season; they transgressed this command, and sin and misery came into the world.

3. The Consequences of the Fall.—"Sin, when it is completed, begetteth death," says St. James (1,15). The dreadful effects of sin are seen in our first parents. By their pride and disobedience they *forfeited all their supernatural gifts,* were expelled from Paradise, and became liable to eternal damnation. They did not lose the natural image of God, but their *understanding was darkened* and their *will weakened.* They became subject to sickness, suffering and death.

Even if Adam and Eve had not sinned, says St. Thomas, and lost the gifts destined for their descendants, still each one of their descendants, being endowed with understanding and free will, would have had to undergo a trial similar to theirs.

SUGGESTIONS FOR STUDY AND REVIEW

1. Show how our souls resemble God and how they differ from Him.
2. How were our first parents *supernatural images* of God?
3. What special privileges did our first parents enjoy?
4. What is meant by the *Golden Age* of the world?
5. To what trial were our first parents subjected? Analyze their sin.
6. What ancient myths preserve the tradition of the Fall?
7. What were the effects of the sin of our first parents?
8. Would each one of us have to undergo a trial similar to that of our first parents even if they had not sinned? Why?
9. Copy the following texts: Apoc. 12,9 and 20,2. What do you learn from them about the serpent who tempted Eve?
10. *Reading:* Conway, *Question Box,* pp. 219-220.

CHAPTER VIII

Original Sin

"By one man sin entered into this world, and by sin death; and so death passed upon all men, because all had sinned."—Rom. 5,12.

1. Why Adam's Sin Is Called Original Sin.—Adam, as we have seen, had received sanctifying grace and the other supernatural gifts, not for himself alone, but also for all his descendants. Hence, by his disobedience he plunged the whole human race into the greatest misery. Sin, with all its disastrous consequences, passed from Adam to all mankind, so that we all came into this world infected with sin. We call this sin *Original Sin*, because we have not actually committed it, but have inherited it from our first parent who was the *origin* or source of all mankind. If the source is tainted, the water flowing from it is also tainted.

2. The Teaching of Scripture on Original Sin.—Holy Scripture clearly teaches that all men are born with the stain of Original Sin upon them: "By one man sin entered into this world, and by sin death; and so death passed upon all men, because all had sinned. . . . Therefore, as by the offense of one, unto all men came condemnation; so also by the justice of one, unto all men comes justification" (Rom. 5,12,16). St. Paul compares Christ with Adam: Sin and death came by Adam; grace and life by Christ, the second Adam. In another place St. Paul says: "We were by nature children of wrath" (Eph. 2,3).

3. Original Sin and Tradition.—The doctrine of Original Sin has always been taught in the Church. The heretic Pelagius taught that Adam by his sin had merely given bad example to his descendants. St. Augustine wrote against him in defense of the Catholic doctrine. "I have not invented Original Sin," he says, "for the Catholic Church has from the beginning professed belief in it." At the Council of Ephesus (431) the doctrine of Original Sin was solemnly declared to be an article of faith.

The *Baptism of infants*, which was practiced in the Church from the earliest times, and which Origen declared to be of Apostolic institution, would be a meaningless ceremony if those infants were not born with Original Sin, because, as St. Peter says, Baptism is administered for the remission of sins (Acts 2,38).

4. Original Sin a State, Not an Act.—Original Sin is a *sinful state* in which every descendant of Adam is born into this world. It consists above all in the *absence of sanctifying grace.* Instead of being born with sanctifying grace and therefore holy and pleasing to God, we are born in the same state in which Adam was after his fall. This state is displeasing to God, because He did not wish it, and for this reason it is called *sin.* Hence Original Sin, though not actually committed by us, is nevertheless truly sin.

"We, as the children of Adam, are heirs to the consequences of his sin, and have forfeited in him that spiritual robe of grace and holiness which he had given him by his Creator at the time that he was made. *In this state of forfeiture and disinheritance we are all of us conceived and born.*"

—NEWMAN.

5. Original Sin and Baptism.—Sanctifying grace and the right of inheriting the Kingdom of Heaven is restored to man by the Sacrament of Baptism; but the other *consequences of Original Sin* remain after Baptism—the darkening of the understanding, the inclination of the will to do evil (concupiscence), and all sorts of hardships, pains, sickness and death.

Those who die with the stain of Original Sin upon them cannot see the face of God in Heaven, but they do not suffer the pains of Hell unless they have committed grievous sin themselves and have died without repenting of it.

6. Importance of the Doctrine of Original Sin.—The history of mankind and of each human individual is unintelligible to those who do not believe in Original Sin. The doctrine of Original Sin alone explains the many riddles of our lives. It tells us why our wills are so prone to evil; why we fall so easily in temptation and rise again with such difficulty; why we must fight continually if we wish to remain good and advance in perfection; why we must avoid the occasions of sin. Original Sin alone explains why this world with all its beauty and loveliness is and will always be a "vale of tears." Any educational system that does not take into consideration Original Sin and its dire consequences is doomed to failure.

SUGGESTIONS FOR STUDY AND REVIEW

1. How did Adam's sin affect his descendants?
2. Prove the doctrine of Original Sin from Scripture and Tradition.

3. Why do we say that Original Sin is a sinful state?

4. What effects of Original Sin are not removed by Baptism?

5. Why is the doctrine of Original Sin of such great importance?

6. The following objection is often raised against the doctrine of Original Sin: "How can little children, who come into the world without the use of reason, be guilty of sin?"—To answer this objection, distinguish between sin as an *act* and the inherited *penalty* of sin. In former times a nobleman who was convicted of high treason was not only punished himself, but he also forfeited his title of nobility for his descendants. The title of nobility of the first man was: "Child of God and Heir of Heaven." By his *treason* against God, he lost this title for himself and his descendants.

7. Another objection: "How can a sin be handed down or inherited?" Answer by showing how the sins of parents are, in a sense, daily inherited by their children. For example, a man squanders his fortune by drink and evil living, and perhaps contracts some loathsome infectious disease; his children and children's children suffer from the consequences, perhaps forever.

8. "But is it not an injustice on the part of God to impute to us another's personal sin?" We answer: *God does not impute another's sin to us.* Luther said He did, but Luther was wrong. It is only from the *effects* of Adam's personal sin that we suffer.

9. Criticize the following statement: "By their sin Adam and Eve lost the *natural image of God* in their souls."

10. *Reading:* Owen Francis **Dudley**, *Will Men Be Like Gods?* Ch. X, "The World's Tragedy."

CHAPTER IX

The Immaculate Conception

"On Thee, O Lord, there is no spot, and no stain is on Thy Mother."—
St. Ephrem, *Father and Doctor of the Church.*

1. What Is Meant by the Immaculate Conception.—In view
of the merits of her Divine Son, the Blessed Virgin, alone of all
the descendants of Adam, was by a particular grace and privilege
preserved from the stain of Original Sin. This privilege is called
her *Immaculate Conception.*

Since the fall of Adam, all mankind, as we have seen, are
conceived and born in sin. But Mary never was in this state; she
was by the eternal decree of God exempted from it. "It was
decreed, not that she should be *cleansed* from sin, but that she
should, from the first moment of her being, be *preserved* from sin;
so that the Evil One never had any part in her. Therefore she
was a child of Adam and Eve as if they had never fallen; she did
not share with them their sin; she inherited the gifts and graces
(and more than those) which Adam and Eve possessed in
Paradise" (Newman).

2. Definition of the Dogma.—The doctrine of the Immaculate Conception of the Blessed Virgin was solemnly declared to be
an article of the Catholic faith (dogma) by Pope Pius IX.
December 8, 1854. The Pope did not proclaim a *new* doctrine.
No one, not even the Pope, can add to Revelation. That was
given once for all; but as time goes on, what was given once for all
is understood more and more clearly. The Pope merely declared
that the doctrine of the Immaculate Conception was contained in
Holy Scripture and Tradition, and therefore revealed by God.
"Catholics have not come to believe it because it was defined,
but it was defined because they believed it."

The doctrine of the Immaculate Conception is nowhere
expressly taught in the Scriptures, but Pius IX cites two passages
from which it may be inferred, if they are considered in the light
of Catholic tradition. The first is found in Gen. 3,15: "God said
to the serpent: . . . I will put enmities between thee and the

THE IMMACULATE CONCEPTION
Murillo's Famous Masterpiece

woman, and thy seed and her seed; she shall crush thy head, and thou shalt lie in wait for her heel." The woman is Mary, the serpent is the Evil One (Apoc. 12,9). By her Son, Jesus Christ, Mary crushes the serpent's head; that is, breaks his power. "Thus there was *war* between the woman and the serpent, the Scripture says. This can only mean that the woman had nothing to do with sin; for, so far as anyone sins, he is not at war with the devil, but has an alliance with him" (Newman). The second text is the words of the Archangel Gabriel at the Annunciation: "Hail, full of grace, the Lord is with thee; blessed art thou among women" (Luke 1,28). Mary possessed the *fullness* of grace, hence surely also sanctifying grace, from the first moment of her existence.

Many testimonies of the Fathers of the early Church could be quoted which show what a unique position she was universally believed to hold. They call her the second Eve, and extol her perfect purity and freedom from sin—expressions which would not be true if she had been conceived in Original Sin.

St. Ephrem (d.373) says that Mary "was as innocent as Eve before her fall, a virgin most estranged from every stain of sin, more holy than the Seraphim, ever in body and in mind intact and immaculate." And, addressing Christ, he says: "Thou and Thy Mother, you are the only ones that are beautiful in every respect; for on Thee, O Lord, there is no spot, and no stain is on Thy Mother."

A feast called the Feast of the *Conception of Mary* was celebrated in the East as early as the seventh century; in the West it was kept from the eleventh century on. At present the Feast of the Immaculate Conception is celebrated on December 8th as a holy-day of obligation. It is the patronal feast of the Church in the United States.

3. An Argument from Reason.—Our reason tells us that it was *eminently fitting* that the Mother of God should never, even for a single instant, have been under the power of the arch-enemy of God. Our reason also tells us that God *could* preserve Mary from Original Sin. Hence we conclude that He *did*. *Potuit, decuit, ergo fecit,* as they used to say in the Middle Ages.

SUGGESTIONS FOR STUDY AND REVIEW

1. What is meant by the *Immaculate Conception*?
2. Did Pius IX proclaim a new doctrine when he declared that the Blessed Virgin was conceived without sin? Explain.
3. Is the doctrine of the Immaculate Conception found in Scripture?
4. What do the Fathers of the Church say about the Blessed Virgin?
5. Copy the text Apoc. 12,1. What famous painting was suggested by this text?
6. Does the doctrine of the Immaculate Conception deny that Mary owed her salvation to the death of her Son?
7. *Readings:*
   a) Conway, *The Question Box*, pp. 358-360.
   b) Newman, *Meditations and Devotions*, pp. 115-128.
   c) John L. Stoddard, *Rebuilding a Lost Faith*, pp. 178-179.

CHAPTER X

Promise of a Redeemer and Preparation for His Coming

"Man could sell himself into slavery, but he could not ransom himself."
—St. Augustine.

1. Need of a Redeemer.—By their sin our first parents lost sanctifying grace for themselves and their descendants, and fell into the slavery of sin. It was as impossible for them or their descendants by their own efforts to arise from their fall, as it is for a dead man by his own efforts to return to life again. Man of himself could neither atone for the offense he had committed against God nor regain sanctifying grace and the right to Heaven. No one but God Himself can fully atone for an offense committed against the infinite majesty of God.

But God could not make satisfaction *in His own nature.* For satisfaction means reparation in word or deed by *submission* and *self-abasement,* and God is incapable of submission or self-abasement in His own nature.

Therefore, if God required complete satisfaction from men for the offense committed against Him, a Divine Person had to become man and in His human nature make that satisfaction.

And this, God in His infinite goodness and mercy determined to do. He promised fallen man a Divine Redeemer, who was to render full satisfaction in his stead and restore sanctifying grace to him and the right of inheriting the Kingdom of Heaven.

2. Promise of a Redeemer.—The promise of a Redeemer was made immediately after the Fall. God said to the serpent: "I will put enmities between thee and the woman, and thy seed and her seed; she shall crush thy head, and thou shalt lie in wait for her heel" (Gen. 3,15).

The "seed of the woman" is evidently the Promised Redeemer, through whom the power of the devil is to be destroyed and the whole human race freed from subjection to him. The words of promise are called the "First Gospel," because they are the first glad tidings of a Redeemer to come.

THE PROMISE OF A REDEEMER

"I will put enmities between thee and the woman, and thy seed and her seed: she shall crush thy head, and thou shalt lie in wait for her heel." (Gen. 3,15.)

3. The Coming of the Redeemer Delayed.—In order that man might learn by experience the evil and misery of sin, the coming of the promised Redeemer was delayed for many thousands of years. Still, His redeeming work was begun from the moment of the promise. Those who lived before His actual coming could not, it is true, enter Heaven, but with the grace which God gave them on account of the Redeemer to come, they could merit the eternal kingdom and then enter into it with Him.

The place where the souls of the just who died before the work of Redemption was accomplished were detained is called in the Bible *Paradise* (Luke 23,43); Abraham's Bosom (Luke 16,22), and the *Prison of the Just* (1 Pet. 3,19). In the Creed it is called *Hell*, and in Catholic tradition *Limbo*, from the Latin word *limbus*, a fringe or edge, because it was supposed to be located beneath the earth and on the outskirts of Hell.

4. Preparation of the World for His Coming.—In order that the true faith and hope in the future Redeemer might not vanish entirely from the earth, God chose Abraham and made a special covenant with him that the Messias should be born of his posterity. He also distinguished Abraham and his descendants, the Israelites, from all other nations, and from time to time revealed Himself to them in a wonderful manner.

The *Law* which God gave to the Israelites through Moses on Mount Sinai, especially the first of the Ten Commandments, obliged them to remain faithful to the one true God and to abhor all idol worship. The *sacrifices* prescribed in the Law continually reminded them of their sinfulness and of their duty to worship God. The *bloody sacrifices* made them familiar with the thought that the world was to be reconciled with God by blood. Many *Rites* and *Ceremonies*, such as Circumcision, Purification, the eating of the Paschal Lamb, were types of greater things to come.

Later on, God raised up Prophets in Israel, men like Isaias, Jeremias, Ezechiel, and Daniel, who by their preaching and teachings, their threats and admonitions, again and again converted the people from idolatry, and by their prophecies kept alive among them the hope of the Redeemer to come.

God also prepared the *Gentiles* (pagans) for the coming of the Savior. He manifested Himself to them in many ways, exhorting them to penance and amendment, especially by the Israelites whom, with their *Sacred Books,* He dispersed among them: "He hath therefore scattered you [Israelites] among the Gentiles, who know not Him, that you may declare His wonderful works and make them know that there is no other Almighty God besides Him" (Tob. 13,4).

During the Holy Season of *Advent* the Church calls upon us to enter into the feelings of sadness and longing for the promised Messias which filled the hearts of the Patriarchs and Prophets of the Old Testament.

SUGGESTIONS FOR STUDY AND REVIEW

1. Why was a Divine Redeemer needed after Adam's Fall?
2. In what words was the Redeemer (Messias) promised?
3. How was the hope of His coming kept alive among men?
4. How were the pagans prepared by God for His coming?
5. How could anyone be saved before the coming of the Redeemer?
6. *Reading:* The *Proper* of the Masses for Advent and the Advent hymns in your Hymn Book.

CHAPTER XI

Jesus Christ—the Promised Redeemer

"When the fullness of time was come, God sent His Son."—GAL. 4,4.

1. The "Fullness of Time."—At last the great Advent was over. The "Fullness of Time" had come. Then the final promise of the Redeemer was made. An Angel of the Lord brought the glad tidings to Mary in Nazareth. God was about to visit His people; Mary was to be His Mother. "Behold the handmaid of the Lord," she replied to the messenger; "be it done to me according to thy word." *And the Word was made Flesh and dwelt amongst us.*

2. The Names of the Redeemer.—"Thou shalt call His name *Jesus*," the Angel said to Mary, "for He shall save His people from their sins" (Luke 1,31; Matt. 1,21).

Others had borne the name *Jesus,* i.e., "the Lord is help or salvation," but for them it was only a name like any other name; whereas in the Redeemer's case it had a pre-eminent fitness, because through Him the salvation of God truly came to the children of men.

The name of Jesus is the *holiest name.* "God hath given Him a name," says St. Paul, "which is above all names, that in the name of Jesus every knee should bow of those that are in Heaven, on earth, and under the earth" (Phil. 2,9-10).

The name of Jesus is the *mightiest of names.* St. Peter said to the man born lame: "In the name of Jesus Christ of Nazareth, arise and walk; . . . and he, leaping up, stood, and walked, and went into the Temple" (Acts 3,6-8).

The name of Jesus is a *name full of charm and sweetness.* "The name of Jesus," writes St. Bernard, "is honey to the mouth, music to the ear, bliss to the heart." And St. Augustine tells us how his mother, St. Monica, had instilled into his heart a deep love and veneration for the sweet name of Jesus. "The Name of Thy Son," he writes in his *Confessions,* "had my tender heart, even with my mother's milk, devoutly drunk in and deeply treasured; and

THE ANNUNCIATION
"Hail, full of grace, the Lord is with thee: Blessed art thou among women." (Luke 1,28.)

whatsoever was without that Name, though never so learned, polished, and true, took not entire hold on me."

On the Feast of the Holy Name of Jesus, which is kept on the Sunday between the Circumcision and the Epiphany, the Church sings:

> Jesus, the very thought of Thee,
> With sweetness fills my breast;
> But sweeter far Thy face to see,
> And in Thy presence rest.
>
> Nor voice can sing, nor heart can frame,
> Nor can the memory find,
> A sweeter sound than Thy blest Name,
> O Savior of mankind.
>
> O hope of every contrite heart,
> O joy of all the meek;
> To those who fall, how kind Thou art,
> How good to those who seek!

Jesus was the "personal" name of the Redeemer; His "official" name was "Christ." The Greek word *Christos* has the same meaning as the Hebrew word *Messias,* the "Anointed." "We have found the Messias, which is interpreted the Christ" (John 1,41). In the Old Testament the word is used of the High Priest, who was anointed for his office, and of kings, who were also anointed. Hence it was used by the Prophets to designate the King who was to come, the promised Messias.

The early Christians loved to represent Jesus Christ under the *Symbol of the Fish.* The popularity of this symbol was due to the fact that the Greek word for fish, *ichthus,* is an acrostic, consisting of the initial letters of the phrase: *Iesous Christos theou uios soter,* that is, "Jesus Christ, Son of God, Savior." These words clearly describe the character of Christ and His claim to the worship of the faithful. They are a brief profession of faith in the divinity of Christ, the Redeemer of mankind. The Greek abbreviation of Jesus is IHS; of Christ ☒

3. Jesus Christ Is the Promised Redeemer, or Messias. Prophecies and Figures Fulfilled.—In Jesus Christ was fulfilled all that the prophets foretold of the Messias. Jesus said to the Jews: "You search the Scriptures, for you think in them to have life everlasting, and the same are they that give testimony of Me" (John 5,39).

The Prophets foretold the time and place of the Redeemer's

THE BRAZEN SERPENT
An old Old Testament figure of Our Lord's Passion and Death

THE MANNA THAT FELL FROM HEAVEN
An Old Testament Figure of the Church and
the Sacraments

birth; the circumstances of His life, Passion and Death; His Resurrection and Ascension, the sending of the Holy Ghost; the rejection of the Jews and the conversion of the Gentiles; the foundation, spread, and duration of His kingdom, the Church.

All these prophecies were made many centuries before Christ, and were preserved and read by the Jews as divine writings; they were also translated into Greek, and in this way came to the knowledge of the pagan nations.

In Jesus Christ were also fulfilled all the Figures by which the deeds and sufferings of the Messias were foreshadowed in the Old Testament:

The figures of His Passion and Death: *Abel, Isaac,* the *Paschal Lamb,* the *Brazen Serpent;*

The figures of His offices of Priest, Prophet and King: *Melchisedech, Moses, David;*

The figure of His Resurrection: *Jonas;*

The figures of His Church and the Sacraments: the *Ark,* the *Red Sea,* the *Manna,* the *Temple* with its sacrifices.

SUGGESTIONS FOR STUDY AND REVIEW

1. Who is the Promised Redeemer?
2. What do the names *Jesus, Christ,* and *Messias* signify?
3. The following texts will tell you what the Prophets foretold about the Messias, and how those prophecies were fulfilled by Jesus Christ: Matt. 2,6; 1,23; 3,3; 4,13-15; 11,5; Luke 4,18; Matt. 21,4-5; 26,26-29; Luke 22,15-20; Acts 4,11; Matt. 26,67-68; 27,48; Acts 2,29-32; 2,34; 2,17; 11,18; John 16,33; Matt. 16,18; John 18,36. State to what fact in Christ's life each text refers, e.g., Matt. 2,6: the native city of the Messias is Bethlehem, as predicted by the Prophet Micheas, 5,2.
4. Which were the most remarkable *Figures* of the Messias? Show how they were fulfilled in Christ. Figures (Types) are persons, things, actions and events of the Old Testament ordained by God to foreshadow the future (St. Thomas). Types or figures are "symbolical prophecies."
5. *Readings:*
   a) John 1,18; Luke 1,26-38.
   b) Conway, *Question Box,* pp. 50-51.
   c) *Catechism of the Council of Trent,* Part I, Art. 2: "And in Jesus Christ, His only son, Our Lord."

CHAPTER XII

Jesus Christ—True God and True Man in One Person

"Thou art Christ, the Son of the living God."—MATT. 16,16.

1. JESUS CHRIST IS TRUE GOD

1. The Testimony of the Church.—The Church has always believed that *Jesus Christ is true God and of one substance with God the Father.* For this belief the holy Martyrs joyfully suffered tortures and death, and God often confirmed their faith by undeniable miracles.

One of these miracles is particularly remarkable. When Hunneric, king of the Arian Vandals, who most cruelly persecuted those who professed the divinity of Christ, had the tongues of the Catholics of the city of Tipasa, in Africa, torn out, they spoke without tongues as fluently and distinctly as before, and proclaimed everywhere that Jesus Christ is true God. About sixty of them escaped to Constantinople, where all the people saw them and heard them speak daily. This happened in 484, and is attested by many eye-witnesses, amongst others by Bishop Victor of Vita and the philosopher Aeneas of Gaza.

The pagans accused the early Christians of worshiping a crucified God. In the year 1856 a caricature of the Crucifixion was discovered on a wall in the palace of the Roman Emperors on the Palatine. It represents a Christian worshiping a crucified figure with an ass's head. Beneath the figure are scratched the words: "Alexamenos worships his· God." Pliny the Younger, the Roman governor of Bithynia in Asia Minor, wrote to the Emperor Trajan in the year 112, that the Christians in their meetings "sing hymns to Christ as to a God."

During the persecution of Decius (A.D. 250) Polemon, the Roman judge, asked a Christian woman: "What God dost thou adore?" She answered: "The almighty God who made heaven and earth." Immediately afterwards he asked another Christian: "What God dost thou adore?" He answered: "Christ." "What," said the Judge, "is that another God?" "No," replied the Christian, "He is the same God whom my companion has confessed."

At the Council of Nicaea (A.D. 325) the Church solemnly defined the Divinity of Christ in the following terms: "*I believe in one Lord Jesus Christ, the only-begotten Son of God, and born of the Father before all ages; God of God, Light of Light, true*

114

God of true God; begotten, not made; consubstantial with the Father."

PAGAN CARICATURE OF THE CRUCIFIXION

2. The Testimony of the Apostles.—The belief of the Church is founded on the belief of the Apostles. The Apostles teach explicitly:

a) That Jesus Christ is true God. "We know that the Son of God is come," says St. John. "This is the true God and eternal life" (1 John 5,20).

b) That He possesses the fullness of the Godhead and the infinite perfections of God. "In Him [Christ] dwelleth all the fullness of the Godhead corporeally" (Col. 2,8). "In the beginning was the Word, and the Word was with God, and the Word was God. . . . All things were made by Him" (John 1,1-3).

c) That all creatures should adore Him. "In the name of Jesus every knee should bow, of those who are in Heaven, on earth, and under the earth, and every tongue should confess that the Lord Jesus Christ is in the glory of God the Father" (Philip. 2,10-11).

The Apostles proclaimed their belief in Christ's Divinity before all men, worked many miracles to confirm it, and, like their Divine Master, laid down their lives for it.

3. The Testimony of Christ Himself.—Christ testifies that He is the Son of God and true God like His Father:

a) He makes Himself equal to the Father. "I and the Father are one" (John 10,30). "All things whatsoever the Father hath are mine" (John 16,15). "He that seeth Me seeth the Father also" (John 14,9). He declared under oath that He is the Son of God (Matt. 26,64).

b) He claims divine attributes: eternity, omnipotence and omniscience. "Before Abraham was made, I am" (John 8,58). "What things soever the Father doth, these the Son doth also in like manner, . . . for as the Father raiseth up the dead and giveth life, so the Son also giveth life to whom He will" (John 5,19). "Heaven and earth shall pass, but My words shall not pass" (Matt. 24,35).

c) He assumes divine rights and claims divine honors. He claims and exercises the right to forgive sins and to sit in judgment on men. "For neither doth the Father judge any man, but hath given all judgment to the Son, that all men may honor the Son as they honor the Father" (John 5,22).

THE FISH SYMBOL (From the Catacombs)

d) He accepts and confirms the testimony of His Apostles. When Peter said to Jesus: "Thou art Christ, the Son of the living God," and Thomas cried out: "My Lord and my God," Jesus confirmed the faith and the declarations of both Apostles (Matt. 16,16; John 20,28).

4. Christ Confirms His Testimony by the Holiness of His Life as well as by Miracles and Prophecies.—Christ was free from every sin and imperfection, and was so conspicuous for virtue that for all time He must remain the model for all men. He said to the Jews: "Which of you shall convince Me of sin?" and none dared to reply. Judas, the traitor, bore witness to His holiness when he declared: "I have sinned in betraying innocent blood." And Pilate had to admit before all the people, "I find no cause in Him." The Gospels are full of examples of His charity, humility, gentleness, forbearance, patience, clemency, love of His enemies, of the poor, the afflicted, the outcast. . . .

Christ worked numerous miracles, many of them before hundreds or thousands of witnesses, such as the multiplication of the loaves and the resurrection of Lazarus. His own resurrection is the crown of all His miracles and the supreme proof of His Divinity.

Christ foretold events which God alone could know—the betrayal of Judas, the denial of Peter, His own passion and death with all their details, His resurrection and ascension, the destruction of Jerusalem, the rapid spread and duration of His Church, the persecution of His followers. . . .

THE RESURRECTIION OF CHRIST

5. Christ Seals His Testimony by His Death.—The death of Jesus is the surest proof of the truth of His claim to be the Son of God and true God. At His trial the High Priest said to Him: "I adjure Thee by the living God that Thou tell us if Thou be the Christ, the Son of God." Jesus knew that life or death depended on His answer to this question. If He had answered, "I am not

the Son of God," He would not have been condemned to death.
But He solemnly confessed: "Thou hast said it" (Matt. 26,64);
and on account of this confession He suffered death.

We must therefore either accept Christ as the Son of God, or
regard Him as the greatest fool and rascal that ever lived; for
only a person who is mentally unbalanced or filled with devilish
malice could persist until death in calling Himself God if he is
not God.

2. Jesus Christ Is True Man

1. The Incarnation.—When the time fixed by God for the
fulfillment of His promise to send a Redeemer arrived, the Son
of God, the Second Person of the Blessed Trinity, became man
through the operation of the Holy Ghost, and was born of the
Virgin Mary.

THE BIRTH OF JESUS
The Adoration of Our Lord by the Shepherds and the Magi

The Son of God became man means that He took a human
body and a human soul; that He could feel and suffer as we can,

and that He was like to us in all things except sin. "And the Word was made flesh and dwelt amongst us."

Christ had a true *human body*. He felt hunger and thirst, ate and drank, was often weary and footsore, slept, suffered and died. He also had a true *human soul*. He had compassion on the widow of Naim, raised the daughter of Jairus from death, wept over Jerusalem, loved Martha and Mary and Lazarus, rejoiced at the confession of Peter. In the Garden He prayed: "My soul is sorrowful unto death," and on the cross He bowed His head and died with the words: "Father, into Thy hands I commend My spirit."

CHRIST RAISES THE DAUGHTER OF JAIRUS TO LIFE

2. The Man Christ the Ideal of Human Beauty?—During the ages of persecution the Christians generally held that Christ assumed a bodily form "without comeliness or beauty." St. Justin Martyr and other early Fathers speak of Christ as of abject appearance. They based their view on the words of Isaias: "There is no beauty in Him nor comeliness . . . and His look was, as it were, hidden and despised" (53,2-3). After the triumph of the Church under Constantine the Great a different view of Our

Lord's personal appearance prevailed. St. John Chrysostom and St. Jerome regarded Him as the ideal of human beauty, and quoted in support of their opinion the words of the Psalmist: "Thou art beautiful above the sons of men" (Ps. 44,3). This has ever since been the most popular view, and the only one that could be adopted by Christian art. Still, it did not find universal acceptance. St. Thomas, for example, denies that Our Lord's body, before the Resurrection, exhibited any extraordinary beauty. (Cf. *Cath. Dict.,* Art. "Personal Appearance of Christ.")

3. Jesus Christ God and Man in One Person

1. Jesus Christ Is Only One Person.—The Second Person of the Blessed Trinity united the human nature inseparably with Himself. This union is called a *hypostatic, that is, personal,* union.

That Christ is only one Person is clearly taught in Scripture. Both human and divine actions were attributed to Him. "In this we have known the charity of God," writes St. John, "because He hath laid down His life for us" (1 John 3,16). St. John here speaks of the Son of God, and says that He died for us, though He suffered death not in His divine but in His human nature. "I and the Father are one." Here Christ ascribes the divine nature to Himself. One person therefore possesses the divine and human nature, and acts through both.

If there were two persons in Christ, Mary would not be the Mother of God, and Christ would not be God. God would not have died for us, but only the man Christ. *Nestorius,* Patriarch of Constantinople, who maintained that Christ was only the temple of God, was condemned by the Council of Ephesus (A.D. 431).

2. There Are Two Distinct Wills in Christ.—Since there are two complete natures in Christ, it follows that there are two distinct wills in Him: a divine will and a human will. The human will of Christ was, however, always in perfect harmony with the divine will. "If it be possible, let this chalice pass from Me; nevertheless, not as I will, but as Thou wilt."

The Sixth General Council (A.D. 680) condemned the heresy of Sergius, Patriarch of Constantinople, who taught that there was only one, and that a divine will, in Christ.

4. SUMMARY OF THE CHURCH'S TEACHING ON THE INCARNATION

The second part of the *Athanasian Creed* admirably sums up the teaching of the Church on the joyful mystery of the Incarnation. After setting forth the Catholic doctrine of the Trinity, the Creed continues:

"Furthermore, it is necessary to everlasting salvation to *believe faithfully the Incarnation of Our Lord Jesus Christ.* Now the right faith is this, that we believe and confess that our Lord Jesus Christ, the Son of God, is both God and Man.

"He is God of the substance of the Father, begotten before all time; and He is Man, born of the substance of His Mother since the beginning of time: perfect God and perfect Man, consisting of a rational soul and human flesh,

"Equal to the Father according to His Divinity; less than the Father according to His Humanity; who, although He is both God and Man, yet He is not two, but *one Christ*:

"*One,* not by the conversion of the Godhead into flesh, but by the assuming of human nature unto God; one altogether, not by mingling of substance, but by *unity of person.*

"For as the rational soul and the body constitute one man, so God and Man is *one* Christ."

SUGGESTIONS FOR STUDY AND REVIEW

1. What is the testimony of the Church on the Divinity of Christ?
2. What did the Apostles teach about Christ?
3. What did Christ Himself claim to be? How did He prove His claim?
4. How many persons are there in Christ? How many natures? How many wills?
5. Give some examples from Scripture that prove that Christ was really and truly human.
6. There are two views about Christ's human appearance. Which do you hold? Give your reasons for holding it.
7. Name five famous paintings of Christ that you have seen.
8. Why is the *Angelus Bell* rung three times a day? What feast commemorates the Incarnation of Christ? How do we show our reverence for the mystery of the Incarnation at Mass?
9. *Reading:*
   a) Carroll, *The Man-God,* pp. 74-80.
   b) Stoddard, *Rebuilding a Lost Faith,* Ch. VIII, "What Think Ye of Christ?"

CHAPTER XIII

Prerogatives of the Human Nature of Christ

"We saw His glory, the glory as it were of the only-begotten of the Father, full of grace and truth."—JOHN 1,14.

Christ's human nature, being the nature of a Divine Person, possessed all the perfections of which human nature is capable, and which are not opposed to the purpose for which Christ became man. Hence Christ was not exempt from suffering and death, because He wished to redeem us by His passion and death.

1. Christ Possessed on Earth the Vision of God Face to Face, as well as perfect knowledge, directly infused by God, of all natural and supernatural truths. He had knowledge not only of the past, but also of the future. The Prophets had received revelations of some mysteries of God and of some future events, but in Christ there was present the *whole truth.* "I am the Light of the world," He says; "he that followeth Me walketh not in darkness." And the Beloved Disciple says of Him: "We saw His glory, the glory, as it were, of the only-begotten of the Father, full of grace and truth."

2. Christ Was Incapable of Sin.—The power to sin is not a perfection, but an imperfection of the will. Christ's human nature was sanctified, not only by its union with the Second Person of the Blessed Trinity, but also by sanctifying grace. It was, moreover, adorned with all virtues, except the theological virtues of Faith and Hope. He saw God and possessed Him, and hence He could have neither Faith nor Hope.

3. Christ's Human Nature Claims Adoration.—We adore the human nature of Christ, not for its own sake, but because it belongs to a Divine Person. We adore the *whole* Christ, and therefore also His human nature. Of the Whole Christ the Scripture says: "Let all the Angels of God adore Him" (Heb. 1,6).

Christ as man consists of soul and body. His body as well as His soul are united with the Divine Person, and therefore claim our adoration. This adoration extends not only to the whole body,

but also to its different parts—the Precious Blood, the Five Holy
Wounds, the Sacred Heart. . . .

THE SACRED HEART OF JESUS   THE IMMACULATE HEART OF MARY

4. The Sacred Heart of Jesus.—There are various reasons
why the Sacred Heart of Jesus should be especially honored and
adored:

a) Christ Himself points to His Heart as the seat of those
virtues and sentiments which we ought to imitate: "Learn of Me,
because I am meek, and humble of Heart" (Matt. 11,29).

b) The feelings of the soul are in some way manifested in the
heart, or at least exercise an influence upon it. "Thou shalt love
the Lord thy God with thy whole heart," says Our Savior; and
through the Prophet, God says to us: "My son, give Me thy heart."

c) In the languages of all nations the heart is the emblem of
love. The Sacred Heart of Jesus is therefore the symbol of God's
eternal love for us, and for this reason above all we adore it in a
special manner.

d) The Heart of Jesus is a human heart, like ours. "Every
chord of feeling in us (sin excepted) has its answer in the Heart
of Christ. He understands us *all*. So whatever our character and
special difficulties are we can take them to Him."

Private devotion to the Sacred Heart flourished in many parts of Europe
from the twelfth to the sixteenth century, as we know from the lives and writ-

ings of St. Bernard, Bl. Herman Joseph, St. Gertrude, St. Mechtildis, St. Peter Canisius. During the Reformation period it died out almost completely. In the 17th century God raised up St. Margaret Mary Alacoque (1647-1690) to be the apostle of the great modern devotion to the Sacred Heart. Christ Himself made known to her the favors in store for those who practice this devotion. She urged the establishment of the Holy Hour and the practice of receiving Holy Communion on the First Friday of each month. In 1900 Pope Leo XIII consecrated the whole human race to the Sacred Heart. The *Feast of the Sacred Heart* is kept on the Friday after the Octave of Corpus Christi, thus showing how intimately devotion to the Sacred Heart is bound up with devotion to the Blessed Sacrament.

SUGGESTIONS FOR STUDY AND REVIEW

1. Summarize the prerogatives, that is, the special rights and privileges, of the Human Nature of Christ.
2. Why was not Christ exempt from suffering and death?
3. Give four reasons why we should have a special devotion to the Sacred Heart.
4. Tell about the history of this devotion. What is meant by the Holy Hour?
5. Write a paper on the *Litany of the Sacred Heart*, using the following outline:

    1) Litany approved in 1900 by Pope Leo XIII. Indulgences.
    2) Thirty-three invocations. Why?
    3) Christ is true God and true Man, therefore God-Man (Invocations 1-3).
    4) Christ is the God-Man: what follows from this doctrine for the devotion to the Sacred Heart? (Invocations 4-15).
    5) The Sacred Heart of Jesus according to the Scriptures (Invocations 16-30).
    6) Conclusion: The Sacred Heart of Jesus the anchor of our salvation (Invocations 31-33).
6. Look up Rom. 8,22. Do these words of St. Paul explain the invocation: "Desire of the everlasting hills"?
7. *Reading:*
    a) Conway, *The Question Box,* p. 48f.
    b) Newman, *Meditations and Devotions,* pp. 571-574 (*See below*).

CARDINAL NEWMAN ON DEVOTION TO THE SACRED HEART

O Sacred Heart of Jesus, I adore Thee. Thou art the Heart of the Most High made man. In worshipping Thee, I worship my Incarnate God, Emmanuel. I worship Thee, as bearing a part in that Passion which is my life, for Thou didst burst and break, through agony, in the Garden of Gethsemani and Thy precious contents trickled out, through the veins and pores of the skin, upon the earth. And again, Thou hadst been drained all but dry upon the Cross; and then, after death, Thou wast pierced by the lance, and gavest out the small remains of that inestimable treasure, which is our redemption.

My God, my Savior, I adore Thy Sacred Heart, for that Heart is the seat and source of all Thy tenderest human affections for us sinners. It is the instrument and organ of Thy love. It did beat for us. It yearned over us. It was on fire through zeal that the glory of God might be manifested in and by us. It is the channel through which has come to us all Thy overflowing human affection, all Thy Divine Charity towards us. All Thy incomprehensible compassion for us, as God and Man, as our Creator and our Redeemer and Judge, has come to us, in one inseparably mingled stream, through that Sacred Heart. O most Sacred symbol and Sacrament of Love, divine and human, in its fulness, Thou didst save me by Thy divine strength, and Thy human affection, and then at length by that wonderworking blood, wherewith Thou didst overflow.

O make my heart beat with Thy Heart. Purify it of all that is earthly, all that is proud and sensual, all that is hard and cruel, of all perversity, of all disorder, of all deadness. So fill it with Thee, that neither the events of the day nor the circumstances of the time may have power to ruffle it; but that in Thy love and Thy fear it may have peace.

CHAPTER XIV

Mary, the Mother of the Redeemer

"Blessed art thou among women, and blessed is the Fruit of thy womb."
—LUKE 1,42.

1. Mary, the Mother of God.—The Blessed Virgin Mary is truly the Mother of God, because her Son Jesus is not only man, but also God. Just as Holy Scripture says: "God has given His life for us," so we can truly say: "God was born of the Virgin Mary," not indeed according to His divinity, but according to His humanity. Elizabeth greeted Mary as the Mother of God. "Whence is this to me," she says, "that the *Mother of my Lord* should come to me?"

Since the third century the title of Mother of God has been given to the Blessed Virgin in the whole Church. *Nestorius,* who denied her this title, was condemned by the Council of Ephesus (431 A.D.). "Whoever does not confess," the Council declared, "that the Emmanuel is truly God, and therefore the Blessed Virgin truly the Mother of God, let him be anathema."

2. Mary Co-operated in the Redemption.—In the realm of grace God does nothing without the consent of the creature. Man must co-operate with the grace of God if he wishes to be saved. In the same way God sought the co-operation of one of His creatures when He carried out His plan to redeem the world. This creature was Mary. The first act of Mary's co-operation in the work of Redemption was her consent to become the Mother of the Redeemer. "As Eve, through disobedience and disbelief, became the handmaid of the devil in the work of destruction, even so Mary, through obedience and faith, became the handmaid of God in the work of restoration." Mary replied to the Angel's message: "Behold the handmaid of the Lord, be it done to me according to thy word." It was only then that the Word could become Flesh, that is, assume a human body through the operation of the Holy Ghost.

3. Mary's Divine Motherhood the Source of All Her Graces and Privileges.—Immediately after Jesus comes His Mother Mary. The distance between them is indeed infinite, for Jesus is God, and Mary is but the creature of His hands. Yet Mary comes

THE VISITATION

"And Mary rising up in those days, went into the hill country with haste into a city of Juda." (Luke 1,39.)

nearest to Jesus, and is therefore the First of creatures in the orders of grace and of glory. "The nearer a thing approaches to its source," says St. Thomas, "the more does it partake of the effect of that source . . . ; but Christ is the source, the principle of grace, and Mary is nearest to Him, since He received from her His human nature. Hence she ought to receive from Christ a greater fullness of grace than any other creature." From her Divine Motherhood proceed all her graces and privileges: her Immaculate Conception, her sinless perfection, her incomparable glory in Heaven, her marvelous intercessory power.

Because in dignity, sanctity and glory Mary excels all God's creatures, a *higher degree of veneration,* above all Angels and Saints, is due her; and because her intercession is more powerful than theirs, she deserves to be invoked above all the Angels and Saints. She is the *Queen of All Saints.*

4. An Objection Answered.—It is foolish to say that by venerating the Blessed Virgin so highly we detract from the honor and glory we owe to God. Why do we love her and honor her? Because she is the Mother of God; because the King of

Angels became her Son; because the heart that shed its last drop of blood for us was formed of her flesh and blood. It is God, therefore, whom we glorify by every word that we speak in Mary's praise. All the glories of Mary are for the sake of her Son. "We praise and bless her as the first of creatures, that we may duly confess Him as our sole Creator."

5. Mary's Assumption.—It is the universal belief of the Church that the body of the Blessed Virgin was gloriously assumed into Heaven immediately after her death. As early as the sixth century the Feast of the Assumption was celebrated on the 15th of August. "It was surely fitting," says Cardinal Newman, "it was becoming, that she should be taken up into Heaven and not lie in the grave till Christ's second coming, who had passed a life of sanctity and of miracle such as hers. Why should she share the curse of Adam, who had no share in His fall?"

THE ASSUMPTION OF THE BLESSED VIRGIN

Holy Scripture repeatedly speaks of the *brothers of Jesus*. In the Gospel of St. Matthew they are called James, Joseph, Simon and Jude. But they were only near relatives of Jesus, probably from His Mother's side. The word "brother" is often used in the Bible for "relative." Thus Abraham said to his nephew Lot: "We are brothers." St. John (19,25) mentions a certain Mary of Cleophas as the sister of the Blessed Virgin, but as two sisters would hardly have the same name, she was probably only a near relative of the Mother of Jesus. It is this Mary who is mentioned by St. Matthew (27,56) as the mother of James and Joseph.

Jesus is called in the Gospels the "first-born son" of Mary. That does not mean that Mary had other children besides Jesus. In the Epistle to the Hebrews (1,6) Christ is called the *first-begotten* of the Father, but surely that does not mean that there is more than one Son of God. The word *first-born* is used in Scripture also for *only-begotten.* It was a title of distinction, because according to law the first-born males were consecrated to God.

St. Joseph
Patron of the Universal Church.

6. St. Joseph, Spouse of Mary and Foster-Father of Jesus.—St. Joseph was chosen by God to be the spouse of Mary and the foster-father of Jesus. As such he had all the rights and

duties of a true father, and Jesus, we are told, was subject to Him. His exalted dignity, his holiness—Scripture calls him a *just man* —his faith and obedience, his blessed death, his power in Heaven, where He now reigns who was obedient to him on earth: such are the reasons why St. Joseph deserves to be especially honored by us, and why we should place confidence in his intercession. To him, says St. Bernard, was granted the honor which kings and prophets sighed for in vain: he might take his Lord and God into his arms, kiss Him, speak with Him, clothe Him, protect Him.

St. Bernardine of Siena and St. Teresa were especially active in promoting devotion to St. Joseph. St. Teresa assures us that she never prayed to him without being heard. In 1870 Pius IX placed the whole Church under the special protection of St. Joseph. St. Joseph is also the patron of workingmen and, very appropriately, of a happy death, since he himself died in the arms of Jesus and Mary.

SUGGESTIONS FOR STUDY AND REVIEW

1. What is the source of all the privileges and graces of the Blessed Virgin? Explain.
2. Explain the expression: "The glories of Mary are for the sake of her Son."
3. Who were the "brothers of Jesus"?
4. Give some reasons why we should pay special honor to St. Joseph.
5. How many feasts of St. Joseph are kept in the Church?
6. Acquaint yourself with the *History of Devotion to the Blessed Virgin*: (a) *Feasts* of the Bl. Virgin; (b) *Hymns* and poems in her honor; (c) famous *churches* dedicated to her; (d) *Saints* who had a special devotion to her; (e) Pilgrimages and *Shrines* of Mary; (f) *Religious Orders* dedicated to her; (g) *Societies*, Sodalities, Confraternities of the Bl. Virgin; (h) famous *paintings*; (i) well-known *prayers* to the Bl. Virgin; (j) *Benefits* resulting from devotion to the Blessed Virgin.
7. *Readings:*
    a) Conway, *Question Box,* pp. 352-356 and 360-368.
    b) Stoddard, *Rebuilding a Lost Faith,* pp. 175ff.

CHAPTER XV

The Work of Redemption Accomplished

"He is the Propitiation for our sins; and not for ours only, but also for those of the whole world."—1 JOHN 2,2.

1. The Redemption, a Great Mystery.—In the beginning of his Epistle to the Ephesians St. Paul describes in simple yet sublime words the mystery of our Redemption:

"Blessed be the God and Father of Our Lord Jesus Christ, who hath blessed us with spiritual blessings in heavenly places in Christ. As He chose us in Him before the foundation of the world, that we should be holy and unspotted in His sight. *Who hath predestinated us unto the adoption of children through Jesus Christ unto Himself* according to the purpose of His will, unto the praise of the glory of His grace, in which He hath graced us in His beloved Son. *In Whom we have redemption through His blood, the remission of sins, according to the riches of His grace*" (1,3-8).

The Redemption is full of profound mysteries. Mysterious is the infinite love of God for man; mysterious the favor shown to fallen man, whereas the fallen angels were consigned to eternal doom; mysterious, in fine, the means of our Redemption: the Incarnation, Passion and Death of the Son of God.

God did not have to redeem fallen man. He could have left him in his fallen state without doing him the slightest injustice. And even after He had determined to restore fallen human nature, He could have done so without becoming man Himself. Only in one respect was the Incarnation of the Son of God necessary, viz., *if God demanded from man a satisfaction or atonement equal to the offense committed by him against the infinite majesty of God.* No creature, neither the holiest man nor the highest Angel, could make such satisfaction. Only a God-Man could offer it.

But even after God had become Man, there were many ways open to Him of redeeming mankind. A tear, a single act of suffering, a single drop of His Precious Blood, as St. Thomas says, would have sufficed to redeem a thousand worlds. He chose, however, to save us by dying for us, by offering Himself on the altar of the cross, a Sacrifice of Propitiation for the sins of the world.

2. The Savior's Sacrifice Was Freely Offered.—The Prophet Isaias said of Him: "He was offered because it was His own will." And the Savior Himself declared: "I lay down My life that I may take it again. No man taketh it away from Me, but I lay it down of Myself; and I have power to lay it down, and I have power to take it up again" (John 10,18). The pagan philosophers of the early centuries sneered at the Christians for worshiping a "crucified God." They thought that Christ had claimed to be a god, but at the decisive moment His divine power had deserted Him. They did not know that He had suffered and died *of His own free will*.

3. Why Christ Chose Suffering and Death.—The Savior chose to undergo the most cruel suffering and to die an ignominious death, the death of a slave and a malefactor, in order to demonstrate before the eyes of the whole world God's horror of sin, as well as God's love for sinners. The Cross of Christ is the eternal monument of Divine Justice and Divine Mercy.

Calvary with its Cross became the "School of Love" where all the Saints meet. Under the Cross mankind learns the divine lesson that the way of the Cross is the only way to victory over sin and sensual desires; the only way that leads to the heights of Christian perfection. "If any man will come after Me, let him deny himself, and take up his cross daily, and follow Me" (Luke 9,23).

4. The Savior's Sacrifice Was Offered for All.—Christ gave His life as a ransom for *all* men, not only for those who will actually be saved. "Christ is the propitiation for our sins; and not for ours only, but also for those of the whole world" (1 John 2,2). Just as God is the God of *all,* so Christ is the Mediator of *all*. Calvin's teaching that Christ died for the salvation of the predestined only, was condemned by the Church.

5. The Fruits of the Redemption.—By His death Christ redeemed us from sin, from the slavery of satan, and from eternal damnation. Christ's atoning sacrifice won for us the right to inherit heaven and all the graces necessary to secure our inheritance. *Our inclination to evil has remained,* but through grace and the virtues infused into our souls together with sanctifying grace we have the power to gain the victory over temptation. *Suffering and disease have remained,* but they have been made to minister to our eternal welfare. *Death has remained,* but "swallowed up by victory" through the certainty of the resurrection. The *Tree of*

He Is the Propitiation for Our Sins. (I John 2,2.)

133

Life has disappeared with the Garden of Eden, but instead of its fruits we eat now the Bread of Angels, the Body of the Lord. God no longer converses familiarly with His creatures as He did in Paradise, but we have instead the sweet companionship of the living, though hidden, Savior in the Blessed Eucharist. Earth is still a "vale of tears," but to the faithful Christian soul it is also a "garden of delights."

6. The Church's Thanks to God for the Redemption.— Daily on a hundred thousand altars the Church's thanks is offered up to God for the work of Redemption. Her banner is the Cross of Christ, the instrument of our salvation. Each year on Good Friday she honors it with most touching and solemn homage. She places it above her altars and on the steeples of her churches, into the hands of her dying children and on the graves of her departed. On Holy Saturday her gratitude for the Redemption finds expression in one of the grandest hymns of praise and thanksgiving ever composed by man:

"It is truly meet and just, that with all our hearts and all our minds, uplifting too our voices, we give praise to Him who is unseen of men, God, the Father Almighty, and to Jesus Christ, His only-begotten Son, our Lord. For, to the Eternal Father, on our behalf, Christ hath paid Adam's debt, and with His own Precious Blood hath blotted out the handwriting set up of old, by sin, against us. Now this is that Paschal festival in which the true Lamb is sacrificed and with His blood the doorposts of the faithful hallowed. This is that very night in which of old time Thou didst bring our fathers, the children of Israel, out of Egypt, making them to pass, dry-shod, through the waters of the Red Sea. This, then, is that night in which a shining pillar of fire chased away the dark cloud of sin and today throughout all the earth calls them that believe in Christ from out of a wicked world and from out of the murk of sin, restores them to Thy favor and clothes them with Thy holiness. This is the night in which Christ the Conqueror broke the chains of death and rose triumphant from the grave! For nothing it availeth us to have been born, save that we were born to be redeemed. O wondrous depth of Thy loving kindness to us! O priceless favor of Thy love! *To save the life of a slave, Thou didst deliver up to death Thy only Son!* Oh, surely, most needful that sin of Adam, since it was to blot it out that Christ died! O happy that fault which won for us so loving, so mighty a Savior! And happy too this night chosen from all others to be witness, in age and hour appointed, of the glory of Christ rising from the dead. It is of this night that it was written: 'And the night shall shine as the day,' and again: 'The night shall be my light in my pleasures.' This hallowed night putteth guilt to flight, washeth sin away, to the fallen giveth back their innocency, and to mourners the joy that had departed. Discord it banisheth; good will it ensureth; the pride of evil it humbleth in the dust."

CHRIST IS TAKEN FROM THE CROSS

SUGGESTIONS FOR STUDY AND REVIEW

1. Review the Life of Christ, dividing it into three periods: (1) His youth and hidden life; (2) His public life; (3) His Passion and Glorification.
2. How was the Redemption of the world accomplished?
3. Why was it necessary that Christ should die *freely* in order to redeem mankind?
4. Could Christ have redeemed the world in any other way than by dying on the cross?
5. Copy the following texts: Matt. 20,28; Mark 14,24; John 10,11; 1 Tim. 2,6; Heb. 9,15. What do they tell you about the Redemption?
6. Is the following statement true or false: "Christ by His preaching and example delivered men from sin"?
7. The following objection is sometimes heard: "Was it just for God to punish His innocent Son for the sins of men?" To answer this objection, remember that Christ suffered *freely*, that He was not punished against His will as criminals are punished, and that God did not look upon His Son as a sinner or as His enemy. *Christ suffered the penalties of sin in order to merit for us the means of making personal satisfaction for our sins;* He transferred His merits to us.
8. What feasts of the Holy Cross are celebrated? What devotions should we practice in honor of the Passion of Our Lord?
9. *Readings:*
    a) The *Improperia*, or Reproaches, of Good Friday in your Missal.
    b) 1 Pet. 1,3-25.
    c) *Imitation of Christ*, Bk. II, ch. 12.
    d) *Cath. Encyclopedia*, "Way of the Cross."

CHAPTER XVI

The Functions of the Redeemer

"I am the Way, and the Truth, and the Life."—John 14,6.

1. The Threefold Office of Christ.—In order to secure the fruits of Redemption, Christ founded a spiritual society, of which He Himself is the Head. He *teaches* its members supernatural truth, *sanctifies* them by His Sacrifice and Sacraments, and *rules* them and leads them on to supernatural happiness. He is therefore at once *Teacher, Priest* and *King.* "To teach holy things, to make and to dispense holy things, and to lead to the enjoyment of holy things"—this is the threefold office or function of the Redeemer, the Head of God's Kingdom.

2. Christ our Teacher, or Prophet.—The Prophets, the spokesmen of God and teachers of Israel, announced Christ as a Teacher of Divine Truth to all mankind. "Behold, I have given Him for a witness to the people, for a leader and a master to the Gentiles" (Is. 55,4). Christ Himself claimed this title repeatedly. "You call Me Master and Lord," He says to His disciples, "and you say well, for so I am" (John 13,13).

Christ is the *most excellent of all teachers.* He spoke as no man had ever spoken, because His human words are the words of a Divine Person. He proved the truth of His words by miracles. His teaching is not merely external: He has power to enlighten and move the minds of His hearers. "I am the Light of the world; he that followeth Me, walketh not in darkness" (John 8,12). He taught by example as well as by words. His whole life is a lesson in holiness.

Christ chose a *poor and humble life,* in order to teach us not to seek after and love inordinately the vain goods of this world, and to be a comforter and model for all the poor and the oppressed. By His word and His example He taught us all virtues in the highest degree, but especially: (1) *Self-denial and Obedience.* "He humbled Himself, becoming obedient unto death, even to the death of the cross" (Phil. 2,8). (2) *Meekness and Humility.* "Learn of Me, because I am meek, and humble of Heart" (Matt. 11,29). He reprimanded the Apostles who were going to call down fire from heaven on an ungrateful town. He washed the feet of His Apostles. (3) *Patience,* Kind-

CHRIST, OUR TEACHER

ness and Mercy even towards His greatest enemies. "A new commandment
I give unto you, that you love one another as I have loved you" (John
13,34). "But I say to you: Love your enemies" (Matt. 5,44).

3. Christ Our High Priest.—Christ is the High Priest of
mankind, the supreme mediator between God and men. "Thou
art a Priest forever according to the order of Melchisedech"
(Ps. 109,4). He delivered Himself for us, says St. Paul, "an
oblation and a sacrifice to God for an odor of sweetness"
(Eph. 5,2).

By this holiest of all sacrifices He delivered us from sin, from
the bondage of Satan, and from eternal damnation, and merited
for us sanctifying grace, adoption as children of God and the
right to eternal happiness in Heaven. Through the merits of His
Passion He, on the day of His ascension, opened Heaven "to all
who believe." At the throne of His heavenly Father He continually
intercedes for us through His Five Sacred Wounds; while here
on earth He continues and applies His sacrifice in the Holy Mass,
thus remaining a Priest forever.

4. Christ Our King.—Both in the Old and the New Testament
Christ is called "King of Mankind," and as such He possesses
legislative, judicial and *punitive* powers. The Angel Gabriel said
to Mary: "The Lord God shall give unto Him the throne of David
His father, . . . and of His kingdom there shall be no end" (Luke
1,32f.). And He could truly say of Himself: "All power is given
to Me in Heaven and in earth" (Matt. 28,18).

Although He is, in the full sense of the words, "King of kings
and Lord of lords" (Apoc. 19,16), Christ is no earthly potentate,
but, as St. Peter says, "the shepherd and bishop of our souls"
(1 Pet. 2,25). Hence when Pilate asked Him: "Art Thou a king?"
He replied: "I am a king; but My kingdom is not of this world"
(John 18,36). And yet it is *in* this world—"a Kingdom of *Truth*
revealed by God, of *Life*, where God lives in His creatures by
Holiness and *Grace*; a Kingdom of *Justice and Love and Peace*,
where men's relations with each other are regulated by their
relations with God" (See the *Preface* for the Feast of Christ the
King).

5. Our Duties to Christ the King.—At the close of the Great
Jubilee year 1925, His Holiness Pope Pius XI proclaimed the new
Festival of the Kingship of Christ to be celebrated throughout the
world on the last Sunday of October. The purpose of the feast is

JESUS CHRIST, KING

". . . all peoples, tribes and tongues shall serve him: his power is an
everlasting power that shall not be taken away: and his kingdom that shall
not be destroyed (*Dan. VII, 14*) . . . and he hath on his garment and on
his thigh written: KING of Kings and, LORD of Lords" (*Apoc. XIX, 16*).

"to bring home to all mankind the fact that Christ is King not merely over individuals, but over *families and societies*, over *States and nations,* over *rulers and tribunals* as well. The duty of Catholics is to hasten the return of the world to His authority by their prayers, their influence, and their actions. They are reminded that they must courageously fight under His royal banner, with the weapons of the spirit, for the rights of God and of His Church."

Priests and Kings were anointed in the Old Testament. The very name of Christ tells us that He is *the* Anointed. For His threefold office Jesus was not anointed with oil, but with the power of the Holy Ghost. "God anointed Him," says St. Peter, "with the Holy Ghost, and with power" (Acts 10,38). The anointing of Jesus is therefore the fullness of the Divinity that dwells in Him.

SUGGESTIONS FOR STUDY AND REVIEW

1. Show that Christ is the most excellent of all teachers.
2. Why is Christ called the Great High Priest of Mankind?
3. Show from Scripture that Christ is truly the King of Mankind.
4. How is the Kingship of Christ described in the *Preface* of the Mass for the Feast of Christ the King?
5. Carefully read the *Litany of the Holy Name of Jesus*. Which invocations refer to Christ our Teacher? our High Priest? our King?
6. Note carefully the use of the expression "Kingdom of God," or "Kingdom of Heaven" by Our Lord. It means, in the first place, "the world-wide Reign of Christ in men's hearts" ("Thy Kingdom come"). Then it also means the Second Coming of Christ and the Judgment. Often there is reference to the *Church*, the instrument by which God's Kingdom is spread. See Matt. 13,1ff. "Parables of the Kingdom."
7. What are our special duties to Christ our King?
8. *Readings:*
    a) The Proper of the Mass for the Feast of Christ the King (Last Sunday of October).
    b) Psalm 2, which describes the victory of the Messias as King over the mighty ones of earth.
    c) Apoc. 19,11-18. St. John describes the triumph of the Christ-King over all the enemies of His teaching, and the victory of the Church at the end of time.
    d) John 17,1-26. The High-Priestly prayer of Christ for His disciples and for all those "who through their word should believe in Him." What graces does He ask for them?

CHAPTER XVII

The Redeemer Living and Working in His Church

"Behold, I am with you all days, even to the consummation of the world."—
MATT. 28,20.

1. Christ Invests His Apostles with His Threefold Office.—
As long as Christ dwelt on earth He personally discharged the
threefold office of *Prophet, Priest and King.* On the eve of His
departure from this world He delegated His powers to His
Apostles. After His ascension into Heaven they and their successors were to teach, to sanctify and to guide mankind. St. Matthew
has preserved for us the memorable words:

"And the eleven disciples went into Galilee, unto the mountain where Jesus
had appointed them. And, seeing Him, they adored Him; but some doubted.
And Jesus, coming, spoke to them, saying: 'All power is given to Me in
Heaven and on earth. Going, therefore, teach ye all nations, baptizing them
in the name of the Father, and of the Son, and of the Holy Ghost: teaching
them to observe all things whatsoever I have commanded you: and, behold,
I am with you all days, even to the consummation of the world" (28,16-20).

From these words it is clear that Christ made His Church the
ordinary medium of salvation for all men. In the Church and
through the Church Christ continues His work of Redemption
till the end of the world.

The Church is the Mystical Body of Christ; Christ as God-Man is the
Head, which animates and directs the body. All Christians should be living
members of this body and thus receive the life-giving influence of Christ.
Hence St. Cyprian says: "Outside the Church there is no salvation. He
cannot have God as his Father, who has not the Church as his mother."

2. How the Church Discharges Her Threefold Office.—
The Church discharges the *Teaching Office* by preserving and
preaching the truths revealed by Christ; the *Priestly Office* by
applying the fruits of the Redemption, the graces merited by
Christ, to each individual soul through the administration of the
Sacraments; the *Pastoral or Kingly Office* by guiding the faithful
through her laws and precepts on the way of salvation.

Christ died for all; still, as the Council of Trent says, all do not reap the
benefit of His death, but only those who make themselves partakers of the

merits of His Passion. "The Passion of Christ is a life-giving remedy; but just as a medicine, though efficacious in itself, profits only those who actually use it, so also the saving remedy of Christ's Passion and Death. God, who procured the means of salvation for one and all, requires our own co-operation." Hence St. Augustine says: "He who created thee without thy doing, does not justify thee without thy doing; He made thee without thy knowledge, but He will not justify thee except by thy own will." It is with the merits of Christ as with the fruits of a tree: they are prepared for all, but no one can enjoy them unless he appropriates them for himself. In order to obtain them, we apply to the Church, the dispenser of the graces of Christ. Only those who have not attained the use of reason can, without their own co-operation, be made partakers of the merits of Christ, as happens in the case of the baptism of infants.

3. Christ and His Priests.—Since the Church is the body of Christ and Christ the Head of the Church (Col. 1,18), the priests are the representatives of Christ, the instruments with which He works. Their sacerdotal acts are the acts of Christ. Hence at the Consecration of the Mass the priest says: "This is *my* Body." Hence, too, when the priest administers a Sacrament, its validity does not depend on his personal holiness. "When Peter baptizes, Christ baptizes," says St. Augustine.

THE LAST SUPPER
"This Is My Body"

4. The Holy Ghost and the Threefold Office of the Church.—In order to enable the Church to exercise her threefold office for the salvation of mankind, Christ not only promised to be with her Himself for all time, but He also promised her the *assistance of the Holy Ghost.* The Holy Ghost was sent to the Church in a visible manner on Pentecost Day, when He came down upon the Apostles in the shape of tongues of fire. The Holy Ghost teaches, sanctifies and rules the Church in an invisible manner until the end of the world. The sanctification of man, which is the chief function of the Church, is also the work of the Holy Ghost. "The charity of God," says St. Paul, "is poured forth in our hearts by the Holy Ghost who is given to us" (Rom. 5,5).

The *Author* of our sanctification is Jesus Christ, because He merited grace for us. The Holy Ghost communicates this grace to us and thus actually brings about our sanctification. For this reason He is called in the Nicene Creed the "Life-giver"; that is, the giver of the supernatural life of the soul.

5. The Work of the Holy Ghost in the Church and in the Souls of the Faithful.—The History of the Church shows us the marvelous results of the work of the Holy Ghost. We see it in the power of the apostolic preaching, in the Inspiration of the Scriptures, in the infallible teaching of the Church and her Head, in the courage of the Martyrs, in the virtuous lives of the early Christians, in the writings of the great Fathers and Doctors of the Church, in the holy and mortified lives of countless monks and nuns, in the unselfish labors of the missionaries in every land under heaven, in the sacrifices made by the faithful for the maintenance of their schools and churches. The working of the Holy Spirit is revealed in the sublimity of Christian art, in the beauty of Christian poetry, in the fertility of Christian charity.

SUGGESTIONS FOR STUDY AND REVIEW

1. Show that Christ invested His Church with His threefold office of Teacher, Priest and King.
2. How does the Church discharge the threefold office delegated to her?
3. What effects did the Holy Ghost produce in the Apostles when He came down upon them on Pentecost Day? See Acts 2,7; and 5,41.
4. Write out the following texts: John 14,26; Acts 15,28; 20,28; John 20,22. What do they tell you about the work of the Holy Ghost in the Church?
5. Why is the Holy Ghost called the "Life-giver" in the Nicene Creed?
6. Is the following statement true or false: "Only a holy priest can administer a sacrament validly"? Explain your answer.
7. *Reading:* the hymns *Veni, Sancte Spiritus* and *Veni, Creator.* What names are given to the Holy Ghost in the second hymn?

CHAPTER XVIII

The Work of Sanctification: Sanctifying Grace

"Know you not that you are the temples of God and that the Spirit of God dwelleth in you?"—1 COR. 3,16.

1. Christ Restores the Supernatural Order.—God, as we have seen, did not give man a merely natural end or destination— a destination which he could attain by the use of his natural powers of understanding and free will. From the very beginning He lifted him up to a share in the life of God, as far as a creature can share it. He destined man to see God face to face and so be happy with Him forever. He made him capable of attaining this destiny by lifting him up to a higher level of life, to a life infinitely above his natural life, to the *supernatural life*. In other words, God set before His rational creatures from the beginning a supernatural end, and placed them in a supernatural relation to Himself, and thus founded what is called the *supernatural order*. Since He was not obliged to do this, and since man had no claim to such a destiny, we call this act of God's love and mercy a *Grace*; that is, a favor or free gift to man. By this grace man is made a sharer in the holiness of God; hence it is called *Sanctifying* (holy-making) *Grace*.

The supernatural order was disturbed by sin. It could only be restored by the still greater mystery of the elevation of human nature to a personal union with the Son of God. By His Passion and Death Christ not only gave adequate satisfaction to God for the sins of men, but also restored the supernatural order by gaining for men the power to be made sons of God and heirs of Heaven. "As many as received Him, He gave them power to be made the sons of God, to them that believe in His name" (John 1,12).

2. What Is Sanctifying Grace?—From what has been said it is clear that Sanctifying Grace is the most wonderful of all God's gifts to His rational creatures. One word cannot adequately describe it. Hence we need not be surprised that Holy Scripture speaks of it in so many ways in order to help us to understand it better. Let us glance at a few of these expressions:

Life: This is the word that Our Lord uses oftenest. "I am come," He says, "that they may have *life,* and may have it more abundantly" (John 10,10). Grace gives to the soul a higher order of life, a godlike life. Because it is above our nature, it is called "supernatural" life. It is also called the "spiritual" life, because it is communicated to us by the Holy Spirit. Mortal sin kills this supernatural life; it is the *"death* of the soul."

Charity: This word, which is of Greek origin and means "love," is used especially by St. Paul and St. John for sanctifying grace (1 Cor. 13; 1 John 4,7ff.). "God is love, and when He lives in us by grace, the first thing that happens is that we begin to love God and our neighbor for the sake of God."

Regeneration: A new or second birth, by which the soul receives a new life from God. "Unless a man be *born again,* . . ." Jesus said to Nicodemus, "he cannot enter into the Kingdom of God" (John 3,5).

Divine Adoption: By sanctifying Grace man is raised from slavery to a share in the family life of God, to companionship with the Son of God. "Behold what manner of Charity the Father hath bestowed upon us, that we should be called, and should be the *sons of God"* (1 John 3,1). "When the fullness of time was come, God sent His Son, . . . that He might redeem them who were under the law, that we might receive the *adoption of sons"* (Gal. 4,4).

Partaking of the Divine Nature: St. Peter (2 Pet. 1,4) uses this sublime expression to describe the new life which men receive through their birth from God. By coming to live Himself in our souls God makes us "partakers of the Divine Nature."

An eminent modern theologian explains, with the help of several apt comparisons, what is meant by the partaking of the Divine nature. "Grace," he says, "penetrates the soul as the glow of fire penetrates the iron. Grace communicates a new quality to the soul, by which it is transformed into the image of God. This new quality is called the new, the higher nature of the soul. As a tree of ordinary kind by the inoculation of a superior bud takes the nature of this bud, and brings forth its blossom and fruit, so our soul is in the highest manner ennobled by the communication of God's grace, which is called in Holy Writ the seed of God, and filled with the power of God, it assumes a divine nature" (SCHEEBEN, *Glories of Divine Grace,* p. 66).

Since Sanctifying Grace is all this—a spiritual renewal, a second birth, a Divine Adoption, a participation in the Divine Nature—it follows that sin is *really destroyed* by it, and not merely *covered over,* as Luther falsely asserted.

3. How Is Sanctifying Grace Conferred Upon Man?—The process by which an adult passes from a state of sin and spiritual death to the favor and friendship of God is called by St. Paul *Justification*. Hence our question is usually put in this way: How is a man justified? The Council of Trent distinguishes *five* steps in the process:

a) God, by His grace, touches the heart of the sinner and calls him to repentance. This grace cannot be merited; it proceeds solely from the love and mercy of God. It is, however, in the sinner's power to reject or to receive the Divine inspiration; it is in his power to turn to God and the practice of virtue or to persevere in sin. Grace does not do violence to his free will, but assists it.

b) Assisted by grace, the sinner on his part voluntarily turns to God and *believes* in the revelations and promises of God, especially in the truth "that the sinner is justified by God's grace through the Redemption which is in Christ Jesus."

c) The effect of this faith is that the sinner is struck with a wholesome *fear* of the justice of God, but at the same time he *hopes* to obtain pardon from the mercy of God.

d) Now he *begins to love God*, hates and *detests* his sins, and *resolves* to lead a life pleasing to God.

e) Thus prepared, he receives the Sacrament of Baptism, or, if he is already baptized, the Sacrament of Penance. If he cannot receive either of these Sacraments, an act of perfect contrition suffices. The sinner has become *just*; that is, he has got himself *right* with God; he is a friend instead of a foe of God, a child of God instead of a slave of the devil. He is numbered amongst those of whom St. Paul says: "You are *washed*, you are *sanctified,* you are *justified* in the name of Our Lord Jesus Christ, and the Spirit of our God" (1 Cor. 6,11).

The process of justification described above refers only to adults. With regard to infants the Church teaches, as we saw before, that they are justified in Baptism without any act of their own.

4. The Indwelling of the Holy Ghost.—It is the Holy Ghost who communicates Sanctifying Grace to our souls. "The charity of God," says St. Paul, "is poured forth in our hearts by the Holy Ghost" (Rom. 5,5). But the Holy Ghost is not only the *Giver* of Sanctifying Grace; He Himself comes into our souls and dwells in them as in His own temples: "Know you not that you are the

temple of God and that the Spirit of God dwelleth in you?"
(1 Cor. 3,16).

Being adopted sons of God, the sanctified must have supernatural powers or faculties to enable them to perform acts befit-
ting their dignity. For this purpose a host of supernatural virtues
are infused into the soul by the Holy Ghost together with Sanctifying Grace. There are, in the first place, the *Theological*, or
Divine, *Virtues* of Faith, Hope and Charity. Furthermore, the
Moral Virtues of Prudence, Justice, Temperance and Fortitude.
These supernatural infused virtues are, as it were, living germs
in the soul which man, with the help of God, can and should develop constantly. The greatest of all these virtues is *charity* (1
Cor. 13).

But even when the soul of man is perfected by the moral and
theological virtues, he still needs to be moved and led by the Holy
Spirit. In order to enable him to follow this movement promptly,
the Holy Ghost bestows *Seven Gifts* upon him: the gift of Wisdom
and Understanding, of Counsel and Fortitude, of Knowledge and
Piety, and the gift of the Fear of the Lord (Is. 11,2).

5. Can We Be Certain of Being Justified?—Without a special divine revelation no one can know for certain that he is justified, though in many cases it may be confidently presumed. "I am
not conscious to myself of anything," says St. Paul, "yet am I not
hereby justified; but He that judgeth me is the Lord" (1 Cor. 4,4).
And in another place he exhorts us to "work out our salvation with
fear and trembling" (Phil. 2,12).

All do not receive Sanctifying Grace *in the same measure*. The measure
is determined by God's benevolence and by their own preparation. Those
who are justified can increase Sanctifying Grace by prayer and good works.
"He that is just, let him be justified still; and he that is holy, let him be
sanctified still" (Apoc. 22,11).

Sanctifying Grace *is lost*, not only by heresy or apostasy from the faith, as
Luther taught, but by every *mortal sin*.

Sanctifying Grace is not diminished or weakened by venial sins. Still they
bring temporal punishment upon us, mar the effects of Sanctifying Grace,
increase our evil inclinations, and prepare the way for the loss of grace by
mortal sin.

SUGGESTIONS FOR STUDY AND REVIEW

1. After Baptism the priest anoints the head of the child with chrism, puts
   a white garment on him, and gives him a lighted candle. What do these

ceremonies signify? Read the prayers said with these ceremonies; they will give you the answer.

2. Prepare a paper, to be read or delivered before the class, on "Sanctifying Grace." Use the following questions for your outline: (*a*) What destination did God give to man when He created him? (*b*) How did He make him capable of attaining this destiny? (*c*) How was the supernatural order lost? How was it restored? (*d*) What expressions does Scripture use to describe Sanctifying Grace? (*e*) How is Sanctifying Grace conferred upon an adult? (*f*) Who communicates Sanctifying Grace to the soul? (*g*) What virtues and gifts accompany Sanctifying Grace? What is the purpose of these virtues and gifts? (*h*) Can anyone be certain of being in the state of grace? (*i*) How can we increase Sanctifying Grace in our souls? How is it lost? (*j*) Which is the greatest gift of God to man? Which is the greatest evil that man can bring upon himself?

3. *Readings:*

  a) *Matt. 22,1-14,* the parable of the Marriage Feast and the Wedding Garment.

  b) Conway, *The Question Box,* pp. 223-225.

  c) Newman, *Meditations and Devotions,* pp. 554-556, "The Paraclete, the Life of My Soul." As this work of Newman may not be accessible, we quote the most striking passages in full:

THE PARACLETE, THE LIFE OF THE SOUL

"I adore Thee, O Eternal Paraclete, the light and the life of my soul. Thou mightest have been content with merely giving me good suggestions, inspiring grace and helping from without. Thou mightest thus have led me on, cleansing me with Thy inward virtue, when I changed my state from this world to the next. But in Thine infinite compassion Thou hast from the first entered into my soul, and taken possession of it. Thou hast made it Thy Temple. Thou dwellest in me by Thy grace in an ineffable way, uniting me to Thyself and the whole company of angels and saints. Nay—as though Thou hadst taken possession of my very body, this earthly, fleshly, wretched tabernacle—even my body is Thy Temple. O astonishing, awful truth! I believe it, I know it, O my God!

"O my God, can I sin when Thou art so intimately with me? Can I expel a Divine Inhabitant by that which He abhors more than anything else, which is the one thing in the whole world which is offensive to Him, the only thing which is not His? Would not this be a kind of sin against the Holy Ghost? My God, I have a double security against sinning; first the dread of such a profanation of all Thou art to me in Thy very Presence; and next because I do trust that that Presence will preserve me from sin. My God, Thou wilt go from me, if I sin; and I shall be left to my own miserable self. God forbid! I will use what Thou hast given me; I will call on Thee when tried and tempted. I will guard against the sloth and carelessness into which I am constantly falling. Through Thee I will never forsake Thee."

St. Catherine of Siena on the Beauty of the Soul
in the State of Grace

St. Catherine of Siena was permitted by God to see the beauty of a soul in the state of grace. Blessed Raymond of Capua, her confessor, asked her to describe to him, as far as she was able, the beauty of the soul she had seen. "My Father," she answered, "I cannot find anything in this world that can give you the smallest idea of what I have seen. Oh! if you could but see the beauty of a soul in the state of grace, you would sacrifice your life a thousand times for its salvation. I asked the angel who was with me what had made that soul so beautiful, and he answered me, "It is the image and likeness of God in that soul, and Divine Grace which make it so beautiful."

CHAPTER XIX

Actual Graces

"Without Me you can do nothing."—JOHN 15,5.

When describing the process of justification, we said that God first of all touches the heart of the sinner and calls him to repentance. Without this *special help of God* nobody could ever get into the state of grace. This help that God gives all the time to everybody is also called "grace," because it, too, is a free gift of God. It is called *actual* grace, because it helps us to perform good *acts* by enlightening our minds and strengthening our wills.

1. The difference between Actual and Sanctifying Grace is this:

a) Actual grace helps us to *do* good, whereas sanctifying grace *makes* us good.

b) Actual grace is a *passing* or transient divine influence upon the soul, a help given us by God at a particular moment to avoid an evil or to do some good; sanctifying grace *remains* in the soul; it is a permanent quality of the soul. Hence we speak of being in a *state* of sanctifying grace.

c) *All men* have actual grace, but only the *just* possess sanctifying grace.

2. The Efficacy of Grace.—The story of the conversion of St. Paul is a good example of the efficacy of grace. Saul persecuted the Christians, arresting them and throwing them into prison. When he was approaching Damascus, a light from heaven shone round about him; he fell to the ground and heard a voice saying to him: "Saul, Saul, why persecutest thou Me?" To his question, "Who art Thou, Lord?", he received the answer: "I am Jesus, whom thou persecutest."

He now saw what a great wrong he had done; *grace had enlightened his understanding.* He immediately resolved to cease persecuting the Christians—*to avoid evil*, and to do what the Lord should ask of him: "Lord, what wilt Thou have me to do?" He did penance, received Baptism, and began to preach the Gospel of Christ—he did good. Grace had *inclined his will to do good.*

THE CONVERSION OF ST. PAUL

3. Necessity of Actual Grace.—Actual grace is necessary before we can begin, or continue, or accomplish even the least work profitable for our eternal salvation. St. Paul declares: "It is God who worketh in you both to will and to accomplish according to His good will" (Phil. 2,13). And in another place he says: "We are not sufficient to think anything of ourselves as of ourselves, but our sufficiency is from God" (2 Cor. 3,5). The reason for this is evident. Eternal salvation is a good of a higher, a supernatural order, and can therefore be secured only by means of a supernatural help. Hence Christ said: "Without Me you can do nothing" (John 15,5).

The necessity of interior supernatural grace was denied by *Pelagius* and his followers in the fifth century. They were vigorously opposed by St. Augustine and St. Jerome.

The *Semi-Pelagians* in the south of Gaul maintained that the *beginning* of salvation is the result of free will, not of grace. They also denied the necessity of grace to persevere to the end in good. Both assertions are false, as we know from the words of St. Paul: "He who hath *begun* a good work in you will *perfect* it unto the day of Christ Jesus" (Phil. 1,6).

Those to whom God has given the grace of *final perseverance* will either not fall into grievous sin any more, or they will at least die in the state of grace.

Without a very special privilege it is impossible even for the just to *avoid venial sins during the whole or even a considerable part of their lives*— "In many things we all offend," says St. James;—this special privilege was granted to the Blessed Virgin Mary.

4. God Gives Sufficient Grace to All Men to Work Out Their Salvation.

—Christ died for all men without exception, and therefore wishes them all to be saved. "God will have all men to be saved, and to come to the knowledge of the truth" (1 Tim. 2,4).

a) To the just God gives the graces necessary to overcome temptation. "God is faithful, who will not suffer you to be tempted above that which you are able, but will make also with temptation issue, that you may be able to bear it" (1 Cor. 10,13).

b) Even the most hardened *sinners* receive graces which, if corresponded with, will bring them back to God. "As I live, saith the Lord God, I desire not the death of the wicked, but that the wicked turn from his way and live" (Ezech. 33,11).

c) The pagans receive sufficient grace to believe in God and to save their souls. They must at least believe "that God exists, and that He is a rewarder to them that seek Him" (Heb. 11,6).

5. God Does Not Give an Equal Amount of Grace to All.

—God distributes His graces to every one according as He wills, giving more to some and less to others (1 Cor. 12,11). We see this from the parables of the Laborers in the Vineyard and the Talents (Matt. 20,1ff. and 25,14ff.). In *prayer,* however, man possesses a powerful means of obtaining more abundant and effectual graces from God. "Ask, and it shall be given you," says Our Lord (Matt. 7,7).

By prayer all graces can be obtained from God, even the grace of perseverance, which cannot in any way be merited. That is why Our Lord insists so much on the necessity of prayer.

6. Grace and the Freedom of the Human Will.

—God's grace does not force the human will, but leaves it perfectly free. It attains its purpose only if man of his own free will co-operates with it. Man can also *resist* grace and through his fault make it inefficacious. Hence St. Paul exhorts the Christian "to receive not the grace of God in vain" (2 Cor. 6,1). Jerusalem was punished because it spurned the proffered graces. "Jerusalem, Jerusalem, . . . how often would I have gathered together thy children as the hen doth gather her chickens under her wings, and *thou wouldst not* (Matt. 23,37).

Cornelius Jansenius (d. 1638 as bishop of Ypres in Belgium) taught that in our present state *internal grace can never be resisted*; in other words, that it is always efficacious. This doctrine was condemned by the Holy See as heretical. *Luther* and *Calvin* asserted that the freedom of the human will had been completely destroyed by original sin.

7. Predestination.—There is a predestination of the elect to eternal happiness. This is clearly taught in Scripture: "God chose us, . . . " says St. Paul, "before the foundation of the world . . . and hath *predestinated* us unto the adoption of children through Jesus Christ" (Eph. 1,4-5). Our reason, too, tells us that there must be a predestination of the elect to glory, for nothing happens, in the natural as well as the supernatural order, without the will of God.

But another question arises: *Is predestination absolute or conditional?* Calvin maintained that God, absolutely and unconditionally, predestined a part of mankind to eternal salvation and another part to eternal damnation. God, he said, wishes some to be good and the rest bad, and for this reason He gives the grace of justification only to a part of mankind, and Christ died only for this part.

This terrible doctrine is evidently opposed both to Holy Scripture and to right reason. God wishes all men to be saved, and Christ died for all; but He foresees from all eternity that many will not co-operate with His grace; these He does not predestine for eternal happiness. Hence *predestination is not absolute and unconditional,* but is based on God's foreknowledge of human behavior. "Those whom He *foreknew,* He also *predestinated* to be made conformable to the image of His Son" (Rom. 8,29). It is absolutely certain that no man is condemned to eternal misery *without his own grievous fault.*

SUGGESTIONS FOR STUDY AND REVIEW

1. What does *actual grace* do for us?
2. What is the difference between actual and sanctifying grace?
3. Do we need actual grace?
4. Does God give His grace to all men?
5. What must we do in order that the grace of God may lead to our salvation?
6. Write out the text *Apoc. 3,20.* Which words in this text refer to actual grace? Which to our co-operation with grace? Which to sanctifying grace?
7. State and briefly refute the errors of Pelagius, the Semi-Pelagians,

Jansenius, Luther and Calvin in regard to grace.

8. Find examples in the Bible which show (*a*) that grace can be resisted; (*b*) that if man co-operates with grace it becomes efficacious; (*c*) that we must pray for grace.

9. How is the different attitude of men towards grace exemplified in the parable of the *Sower* (Luke 8,5-16) ?

10. *Readings:*

    a) *Imitation of Christ,* Bk. I, ch. 25, nos. 1-3; and Bk. II, ch. 10.

    b) *Autobiography of St. Thérèse of Lisieux* (Little Flower), Ch. I, "Earliest Memories" (*See below*).

St. Thérèse of Lisieux on the Unequal Distribution of Grace

"I often asked myself why God had preferences, why all souls did not receive His grace. In reading the lives of the Saints I was surprised to see extraordinary favors showered on great sinners like St. Paul, St. Augustine, St. Mary Magdalen, and many others, whom He forced, so to speak, to receive His grace. In reading the lives of the Saints I was surprised to see that there were certain privileged souls, whom our Lord favored from the cradle to the grave, allowing no obstacle in their path which might keep them from mounting towards Him, permitting no sin to soil the spotless brightness of their baptismal robe. And again it puzzled me why so many poor savages should die without having even heard the name of God.

"Our Lord has deigned to explain this mystery to me. He showed me the book of nature, and I understood that every flower created by Him is beautiful, that the brilliance of the rose and the whiteness of the lily do not lessen the perfume of the violet or the sweet simplicity of the daisy. I understood that if all the lowly flowers wished to be roses, nature would lose its springtide beauty, and the fields would no longer be enamelled with lovely hues. And so it is in the world of souls, our Lord's living garden. He has been pleased to create great Saints who may be compared to the lily and the rose, but He has also created lesser ones, who must be content to be daisies or simple violets flowering at His feet, and whose mission it is to gladden His Divine Eyes when He deigns to look down on them. And the more gladly they do His will, the greater is their perfection.

"I understood this also, that God's love is made manifest as well in a simple soul which does not resist His grace, as in one more highly endowed. In fact, the characteristic of love being self-abasement, if all souls resembled the holy Doctors who have illuminated the Church, it seems that God in coming to them would not stoop low enough. But He has created the little child, who knows nothing and can but utter feeble cries, and the poor savage who has only the natural law to guide him, and it is to their hearts that He deigns to stoop. These are the field flowers whose simplicity charms Him; and by His condescension to them our Savior shows His infinite greatness. As the sun shines both on the cedar and the floweret, so the Divine Sun illumines every soul, great and small, and all correspond to His care—just as in nature the seasons are so disposed that on the appointed day the humblest daisy shall unfold its petals."

CHAPTER XX

Fruits of Sanctifying Grace: Good Works

"Every man shall receive his own reward according to his own labor."
—1 Cor. 3,8.

1. Every Christian Is Bound to Perform Good Works.— Christianity is a Religion of action. In the Sermon on the Mount Christ demands good works from His followers: the eight Beatitudes, Forgiveness of injuries, chastity in thought, word, and deed, almsgiving, fasting, prayer with right intention. At the end of the Sermon on the Mount Christ expressly declares: "Not every one that saith to Me, Lord, Lord, shall enter into the Kingdom of Heaven, but *he that doth the will of My Father* who is in heaven, he shall enter into the Kingdom of Heaven." He cursed the barren fig tree and condemned the servant who had buried his talent. St. James is but echoing the words of his Divine Master when he says: "Even as the body without the spirit is dead, so also faith without works is dead" (2,26).

Before all others we should perform those good works which are enjoined upon us by the Commandments of God and of the Church, as well as those which are necessary or useful to fulfill the duties of our state of life. Holy Scripture especially recommends *prayer, fasting and alms.* "Prayer is good with fasting and alms, more than to lay up treasures of gold" (Tob. 12,8). By prayer we offer up to God our mind; by fasting, our body; by almsgiving, our earthly possessions: by prayer we combat pride; by fasting, sensuality; by almsgiving, avarice—the three great enemies of our souls.

2. Good Works Meritorious only through Sanctifying Grace.—Of themselves our actions are without value or merit for eternal life; they derive their intrinsic value or *meritoriousness* from the infinite merits of Jesus Christ, whose living members we are through sanctifying grace. "I am the vine," says Christ, "you the branches; he that abideth in Me and I in him, the same beareth much fruit; for without Me, you can do nothing" (John 15,5).

Through sanctifying grace we are as intimately united with Christ as the branches of the vine with the parent stem. On account of the sap which they draw from the vine, the branches bear abundant fruit. In like manner the works of the just man receive their intrinsic value from the merits of Jesus Christ. If the branch is separated from the vine, it withers and can no longer bring forth fruit. So also if we separate ourselves from Christ by mortal sin, we cannot perform works meritorious for eternal life. "As a branch cannot bear fruit of itself, unless it abide in the vine, so neither can you, unless you abide in Me" (John 15,4). We lose all our merits when we forfeit sanctifying grace through mortal sin. Theologians, however, assure us that as soon as a sinner does penance and regains sanctifying grace, all his previous merits return to him.

Although good works done in mortal sin are of no value for Heaven, they are not useless. They are very useful to obtain from the divine mercy the grace of conversion, temporal reward or the averting of temporal punishment. The Prophet Daniel said to Nabuchodonosor, the wicked king of Babylon: "Redeem thou thy sins with alms, and thy iniquities with works of mercy; perhaps He will forgive thy offenses" (Dan. 4,24).

3. By Good Works Performed in the State of Grace We Merit:

a) An increase of sanctifying grace. In the parable of the Talents Jesus says: "To every one that hath shall be given, and he shall abound" (Matt. 25,29).

b) Eternal Salvation. "Be glad and rejoice, for your reward is very great in Heaven" (Matt. 5,12).

c) An increase of glory in heaven. "Every man shall receive his own reward according to his own labor" (1 Cor. 3,8). The degree of glory corresponds to the degree of sanctifying grace.

d) The actual graces necessary to preserve sanctifying grace. "Ask, and you shall receive."

4. Good Works and Good Intention.—In our good works God regards less the success we achieve than the efforts we make and the *good intention* with which we act. Our intention is good if we perform our actions in order to serve and honor God. If our intention is good, we may reap a great reward even from the smallest actions. "Whether you eat or drink, or whatsoever else you do, do all to the glory of God" (1 Cor. 10,31).

It is very useful to make a good intention several times a day, but especially every morning. We may say, for instance, "O my God, I offer up to Thee all my thoughts, words and deeds for Thy honor and glory"; or simply: *Omnia ad maiorem Dei gloriam*— All for the greater glory of God!

5. Some Objections Answered.—From what has been said about good works, the objections brought against the Catholic doctrine of merit by Luther, Calvin and their followers can be readily disposed of. How directly opposed to the clear teachings of Christ and His Apostles is, for example, the assertion of Luther that by good works no reward in Heaven can be merited. Luther claimed that the "Popish" doctrine of merit makes God our debtor. St. Augustine had answered this objection a thousand years before Luther made it. "God has become our debtor," he says, "not as though He has received something from us, but because He has promised what pleased Him. It is a different thing when we say to a man, 'You are my debtor because I have given you something,' and when we say to God, 'Give us what Thou hast promised, for we have done what Thou didst command!' "

But does not Our Lord say: "When you shall have done all these things that are commanded you, say: We are *unprofitable servants*; we have done that which we ought to do?" (Luke 17,10). We answer: The parable from which these words are taken is not concerned at all with the question of merit. Our Lord simply wished to teach His disciples, and us, a lesson of humility. Moreover, we are really, as far as our own powers are concerned, *unprofitable servants*: we can perform no meritorious works except with the help of God's grace. "When God crowns our merits," says St. Augustine, "He crowns nothing but His own gifts." We are saved by *grace*, not through *works*, because "nothing of the things which precede Baptism, whether faith or works, merits the grace itself of justification" (Council of Trent).

SUGGESTIONS FOR STUDY AND REVIEW

1. Prove from Scripture that we must perform good works if we wish to be saved.
2. What good works above all should we perform?
3. Whence do our good works derive their value for eternal life?
4. Why cannot a sinner merit by his good works? Are his good works useless?
5. What does a just man merit by his good works?
6. What does a repentant sinner regain together with sanctifying grace?
7. On what does the glory of the Blessed in Heaven depend?
8. Why should we be careful to make a good intention frequently?
9. Refute briefly the false teaching of the Protestants on good works.
10. *Readings:*
    a) Matt. 20,1-17: "The Laborers in the Vineyard."
    b) Conway, *The Question Box,* pp. 226-227, "On Merit."

CHAPTER XXI

Eternal Life

"The just shall go into life everlasting."—MATT. 25,46.

Our faith in God celebrates its grandest triumph in the face of death. Our *Credo* begins with the simple words: "I believe in God," and ends with the jubilant profession of faith in the "resurrection of the body and life everlasting." *Eternal Life* stands in the foreground of Revelation. It is the end for which man was created by God.

THE VISION OF ST. JOHN

1. Eternal Life Consists in the Beatific Vision.—The vision of God face to face—this is the reward promised to the children of God. "Dearly beloved," writes St. John, "we are now the sons of God; and it hath not yet appeared what we shall be. We know that, when He shall appear, we shall be like to Him, because *we shall see Him as He is*" (1 John 3,2). Here on earth we see God only as He is mirrored in His creatures; in Heaven we shall see Him directly, clearly, openly, as He is in Himself. "We now see through a glass in a dark manner; but then *face to face*" (1 Cor. 13,12). In order to enable the blessed to see Him face to face, God enlightens them by the *lumen gloriae*, the "light of glory." To the vision of God is added the possession of God through the bonds of the most perfect love.

2. Some of the Joys of the Blessed.—(*a*) *The ills of life will be no more.* "God shall wipe away all tears from their eyes; and death shall be no more, nor mourning, nor crying, nor sorrow shall be any more, for the former things are passed away" (Apoc. 21,4). (*b*) *Unspeakable happiness is theirs.* "Eye hath not seen, nor ear heard, neither hath it entered into the heart of man, what things God hath prepared for them that love him" (1 Cor. 2,9). (*c*) *They enjoy the Communion of Saints.* They are united in the most intimate love with the glorified Humanity of Christ—it is their eternal Thabor—with His Blessed Mother, the Queen of Heaven, with all the Angels and Saints in the great and holy family of the Church Triumphant. They are united with relatives and friends who went before them in death. As long as the world lasts, they offer up prayers to God for the realization of His Kingdom on earth. (*d*) *Their knowledge will be perfect.* In God they will see all the mysteries of faith and in Him understand all the wonders of creation, the history of mankind and the history of every individual soul; above all, the history of their own progress from grace to glory.

3. The Bliss of Heaven Not Equal in Degree for All.—All the blessed see God face to face, some however more perfectly than others, according to the degree of their merit. "Every man shall receive his own reward according to his own labor," and "he who soweth sparingly, shall also reap sparingly" (1 Cor. 3,8; 2 Cor. 9,6). Yet, in the midst of this inequality, all are perfectly content and happy, rejoicing in one another's happiness and blessing the justice of God.

"One day," writes St. Thérèse in her *Autobiography*, "I expressed my surprise to my sister Pauline that God does not give an equal amount of glory to all the Elect in Heaven—I was afraid that they would not all be quite happy. Pauline sent me to fetch Papa's big tumbler, and put it beside my tiny thimble, then, filling both with water, she asked me which seemed the fuller. I replied that one was as full as the other—it was impossible to pour more water into either of them, for they could not hold it. In this way Pauline made it clear to me that in Heaven the least of the Blessed does not envy the happiness of the greatest. . . ."

SUGGESTIONS FOR STUDY AND REVIEW

1. What does the twelfth article of the Creed teach us?
2. In what does eternal life primarily consist? What is meant by the *Beatific Vision*? By the *Light of Glory*?
3. What are the joys of the Blessed in Heaven?
4. Is the Bliss of Heaven equal in degree for all? If the happiness of some is greater than that of others, how can all be perfectly happy?
5. Is Heaven a place or a state of the soul? (To answer this question remember that Christ ascended into Heaven in that body which He took from Mary, and that Mary herself is body and soul with her Divine Son.)
6. Shall we know our relatives and friends in Heaven? Do the Blessed in Heaven know what is going on here on earth? See Luke 15,10.
7. Copy the following texts: Matt. 13,43; Luke 22,30; Heb. 12,22; 2 Cor. 12,4; Matt. 19,16; James 1,12; 2 Tim. 4,8; 1 Pet. 5,4; Heb. 9,15. What names are given to Heaven in these texts?
8. Reading: *Imitation of Christ,* Bk. III, chs. 47-49.

THE JOYS OF HEAVEN

"How great shall be that happiness where there shall be no evil, no unappreciated good, where all shall be occupied in the praises of God! . . . This shall be our Sabbath Day, not terminated by evening; but the Lord's Day, hallowed by the resurrection of Christ, shall continue a sort of everlasting Octave, betokening eternal rest alike of spirit and body. There we shall have leisure and see; we shall see and love; we shall love and praise. Behold what shall be the end without end. What other is our end but to arrive at a kingdom whereof there is no end?"

—ST. AUGUSTINE, *City of God.*

"Lift up the eyes of thy heart above the earth; love the dear company of the Angels. How blessed the family that dwells there above—where the aged groan not, nor infants cry; where no voice is silent in the praise of the Lord; where neither hunger nor thirst is known, where the heavenly inhabitants are fed with heavenly food; where a royal banquet is spread; where no discord is heard; where life is fresh and enduring and consumed by no fear of death nor any other care. Rejoicing that life's troubles are over, they will look upon the King of Joy: they will reign with Him who reigns, rejoice with Him who rejoices. Then pain and sorrow and trouble shall be no more. Then the King of Kings, the King of Purity, shall be seen of the pure of heart."

—ST. COLUMBAN, *Letter to a Young Man.*

"I pray that Thou wouldst vouchsafe to bring me, a sinner, to that unspeakable Feast where Thou, with Thy Son and Thy Holy Spirit, art to Thy holy ones *true light, fullness of blessedness, everlasting joy,* and *perfect happiness.* Through the same Christ our Lord."

—ST. THOMAS AQUINAS, *Prayer after Holy Communion.*

CHAPTER XXII

Purgatory

"It is a holy and wholesome thought to pray for the dead."—2 MACH. 12,46.

Only those will go straight to Heaven who die free from sin and from all punishment due to sin. Those who still have unrepented venial sins to expiate, or who have not fully paid the debt of temporal punishment due to sins forgiven in this life, are detained for a time in *Purgatory*.

1. There Is a Purgatory.—The existence of an intermediate state between Heaven and Hell was clearly revealed in the Old Testament. "It is a holy and wholesome thought," we read in the Second Book of Machabees (12,46), "to pray for the dead, that they may be loosed from sins."

The Later Jews, as we know from the Rabbinical writings, prayed for the dead and recognized the need of purification after death. Christ and His Apostles made no protest against this Jewish doctrine and practice. Our Lord Himself speaks of "forgiveness of sins in the world to come" (Matt. 12,32), and St. Paul of slight sins to be burned away and the "soul saved so as by fire" (1 Cor. 3,11-15).

A purification of souls after death was known to several pagan religions, such as the Egyptian and the Persian. Plato speaks of souls that have to be cleansed in the river Acheron, because on earth they led but indifferent lives; and of others that have to pass a year in Tartarus (Hell) before they can attain to perfect happiness. He makes a clear distinction between *curable* and *incurable* offenses.

2. The Doctrine of Purgatory Is Most Reasonable.—No one can deny that many die with the burden of venial sin on their conscience, and are therefore unfit for Heaven, because Scripture tells us clearly that nothing defiled can enter Heaven (Apoc. 21,27). But they are not bad enough for Hell either. Consequently there must be a place where they can be made fit for Heaven. "There are some," says St. Augustine, "who have departed this life, not so bad as to be deemed unworthy of mercy, nor so good as to be entitled to immediate happiness." This consideration alone has led many Protestants to return to the ancient custom of praying for the dead. A Protestant had the following words inscribed on the tombstone of a departed friend. "Too bad for heaven, too good for hell, where he went to I cannot tell."

3. The Lot of the Poor Souls.—We call the souls detained in Purgatory the *Poor Souls* because they cannot do anything to shorten the time of their punishment. The precise nature of this punishment has not been defined by the Church. They are certain of their salvation, but they suffer from an intense longing to enjoy that Highest Good, which they now can appreciate as they never could while on earth. It is also commonly held that they suffer a "pain of sense" caused by fire.

4. How We Can Help the Poor Souls.—From the earliest times the Church has prayed for her departed children and offered the Holy Sacrifice of the Mass for them. All the ancient Liturgies, written in many different languages and representing the practice in every part of the ancient world, contain prayers for the dead.

Over many Christian tombs in the first three centuries, both in the Catacombs and elsewhere, we find the phrases, "May God refresh thee," and "Mayest thou have eternal light in Christ." We find the same words used in the Church's prayer for the dead: "Be mindful, O Lord, of thy servants N. and N., who are gone before us with the sign of faith, and sleep in the sleep of peace. To them, O Lord and to all who sleep in Christ, grant, we beseech Thee, a place of refreshment, light and peace, through the same Christ our Lord."

In his funeral oration over the Emperor Theodosius the Great, St. Ambrose of Milan (d.397) prays: "Give rest to Thy servant Theodosius, that rest which Thou hast prepared for Thy saints. . . . I have loved him, and therefore will I follow him unto the land of the living; nor will I leave him until by tears and prayers I shall lead him whither his merits summon him, unto the holy mountain of the Lord."

5. St. Augustine and His Mother St. Monica.—St. Augustine, the greatest Father and Doctor of the Church, devotes the Ninth Book of his *Confessions* to an account of the last days and death of his mother, St. Monica. St. Monica died at Ostia, not long after the conversion and baptism of her son, for whom she had wept and prayed so many years. "When the day of her dissolution was at hand," writes St. Augustine, "she took no thought to have her body sumptuously wound up, or embalmed with spices; nor desired she a choice monument, or to be buried in her own land. These things she enjoined us not; but *desired only to have*

her name commemorated at Thy Altar, from which she knew that
Holy Sacrifice to be dispensed, by which the handwriting that was
against us is blotted out. . . . May she, then, rest in peace with
her husband. . . . And Thou, O Lord my God, inspire thy servants my brethren (the priests), whom with voice, and heart, and
pen I serve, that so many as shall read these Confessions, may at
Thy Altar remember Monica Thy handmaid, with Patricius, who
was once her husband" (*Conf.* IX,13).

6. Importance of the Catholic Doctrine of Purgatory.—
The Catholic doctrine of Purgatory enables us to form some idea
of the glory and beauty of Heaven: in order to enter into the man-
sions of the Blessed even the slightest stain of sin must first be
washed away and the last farthing of debt be paid. For the *living*
the thought of Purgatory is a spur to fidelity in little things, to
earnest striving after perfection, but also a constant invitation to
the practice of unselfish charity towards the souls of the departed.
For the *dying* how consoling it is to know that they belong to the
Communion of Saints and can confidently expect efficacious help
from the Church Triumphant and the Church Militant.

THE SOULS IN PURGATORY
"It is therefore a holy and wholesome thought to pray for the dead,
that they may be loosed from sins."(II Mach. 12,46.)

"Picture to yourselves a soul in purgatory, yearning for prayers, Masses,
and alms to be offered up for him; and instead of that, watching his mourning relatives spending their money on worthless flowers and wreaths to

place above his mouldering corpse! Or putting up a costly monument or raising to his memory an expensive marble head-stone. How bitter and almost insufferable must be the sight of such purely earthly displays of grief to one who has entered into the world of great and eternal realities! One earnest *De Profundis*, or even a single burning ejaculation is, to him, worth more than a whole city draped in black, or an entire churchyard piled with wreaths and exotic flowers. Spiritual help is what the dead seek. The gift of flowers will not assuage their thirst, nor will all the well-known garments and trappings of woe quench the agony that writhes their souls."

—BISHOP JOHN S. VAUGHAN.

SUGGESTIONS FOR STUDY AND REVIEW

1. The definition of the Council of Trent on Purgatory runs as follows: "The Catholic Church, instructed by the Holy Ghost, has from the Sacred Scriptures and the ancient traditions of the Fathers, taught in Sacred Councils, and very recently in this Ecumenical Synod, that there is a Purgatory, and that the souls therein detained are helped by the suffrages of the faithful, but principally by the acceptable Sacrifice of the Altar." Read this passage carefully and then state just what a Catholic must believe in regard to Purgatory.
2. What souls go to Purgatory?
3. How do we know that there is a purgatory?
4. By what means can we assist the Poor Souls in Purgatory? Why are they called *Poor Souls*?
5. Show how important the doctrine of Purgatory is (*a*) for the living; (*b*) for the dying.
6. *Readings:*
    a) The text of the *Mass for the Dead* in your Missal.
    b) The *Burial Service* in the Ritual or in your Missal.
    c) Newman, *The Dream of Gerontius,* sections VI and VII, Description of Purgatory.
    d) Cardinal Gibbons, *Faith of Our Fathers,* Ch. XVI, "Purgatory, and Prayers for the Dead."

CHAPTER XXIII

Eternal Death

"It is a fearful thing to fall into the hands of the living God."—HEB. 10,31.

Eternal Life stands in the foreground of Revelation; but there is also a dark background—*Eternal Death*.

1. Who Will Be Cast into Hell?—All who die in deliberate rebellion against God; that is, with *mortal sin* upon their souls. By mortal sin they completely separated themselves from God; they said to His face: *Non serviam*—I will not serve Thee; they persevered in this state till death, and their separation from God has become eternal. They have brought upon themselves the sentence of the Just Judge: "Depart from Me, you cursed, into everlasting fire" (Matt. 25,41).

The word *Hell* comes from the Old English *hel,* meaning "to cover" or "to conceal." *Hel* was the name of the Scandinavian goddess of the lower world. According to the Edda, all who did not die on the battlefield passed at death to the kingdom of this goddess. Hence it meant in the first place a dark abode or the lower world, the place of the departed spirits. In this sense it is used in the Creed: "He descended into Hell." Then it was used of the place of punishment of the wicked after death. In the Bible the place of the damned is called *gehenna*, the "valley of Hinnom," south of Jerusalem, where, in ancient times, horrid sacrifices were offered to Moloch.

2. The Punishment of the Damned Is Eternal.—The eternity of the pains of Hell is a truth too plainly written on the pages of the Inspired Word to be doubted or explained away. "These shall go into *everlasting punishment*; but the just into life everlasting," says Our Lord (Matt. 25,46). Speaking of giving scandal, Christ says: "If thy foot scandalize thee, cut it off. It is better for thee to enter lame into life everlasting than, having two feet, to be cast into the *Hell of unquenchable fire*, where their worm dieth not, and the fire is not extinguished" (Mark 9,44). Reward and punishment are both eternal according to the clear teaching of Christ.

Origen and others taught that the pains of Hell are not eternal, and that in the end all would be saved. He was condemned by the Fifth Ecumenical

Council (553 A.D.). With two or three exceptions the Fathers and Doctors of the Church are unanimous in teaching the doctrine of an eternal Hell.

3. The Sufferings of the Damned.—In the place of punishment the wicked will experience two kinds of torment: the *pain of loss* and the *pain of sense*.

a) *The pain of loss* is indicated by Our Lord's words: "Depart from Me, ye cursed," and consists in the eternal separation of the sinner from God, and the realization that his failure to reach Heaven is due to his own fault. According to the Fathers of the Church this is the chief punishment of Hell. It is so great a punishment, says St. Augustine, that no torments known to us can be compared to it.

b) *The pain of sense* comprehends all suffering and torment inflicted in Hell, except that which springs from the loss of the vision of God. The term cannot mean pain inflicted on the senses, because separated souls who have no senses are nevertheless subjected to the "pain of sense." Some suppose that this class of suffering is so called because it arises chiefly from a sensible substance, viz., fire. In Scripture the pain of sense is usually represented as fire; but also as "weeping and gnashing of teeth," as "extreme darkness," and as "the worm that dieth not."

"It is undeniable that the expressions used in Sacred Scripture are in a sense metaphors only, and not to be taken literally. But these figures and similes are designed to bring us face to face with the most awful conceptions which the mind of man can entertain, and to implant in us the absolute certainty that Hell is most truly a place of torment. How tremendous must be a reality of which the bare image suffices to strike such fear into our hearts!"

—PESCH, S. J., *The Christian Philosophy of Life.*

Just as the blessed in Heaven will not be equally happy, so neither will the sufferings of the lost be of equal intensity. Each will suffer in proportion to his sins and to his abuse of the graces offered to him. "God will render to every man according to his works" (Matt. 16,27).

4. The Doctrine of Hell and Human Reason.—It is often asked: "Is the doctrine of Hell reasonable or credible?" The great Catholic poet Dante boldly asserts that Hell is a monument not only of justice and power, but of the wisdom and love of God:

Justice the Founder of my fabric moved;
To rear me was the task of Power Divine,
Supremest Wisdom and Primeval Love.
— INFERNO III.

To understand the justice, wisdom, or love which made Hell, is certainly beyond our present ken, says a modern theologian. "To our limited view, Hell, as we conceive it, may seem unjust, unwise, unloving; and attempts to justify it from reason, valid or invalid, may sometimes only irritate us. *Here, if anywhere, we must fall back upon the very notion of faith, as an heroic clinging to God in spite of crushing difficulties*, in spite of all that may appear most contrary to our rooted conviction as to His goodness and mercy. *Eventually I shall surely see how all that was revealed was true.* I am therefore content to wait patiently and trustfully as for the answer to a riddle, which now puzzles me hopelessly because I am on the wrong track for its solution; the more I reason, the faster I stick in the mire. *When I hear the answer, I shall laugh and say, 'Of course! How could it be otherwise?'* "

For the eternity of the pains of Hell our reason furnishes us at least with this one proof, that a Hell which would not be eternal would be of no avail to deter men from committing mortal sin. St. Justin Martyr (d.165) declares that "if Hell does not exist, either there is no God, or if there is, He does not concern Himself with men, and virtue and vice have no meaning." Instead of complaining about the eternity of the pains of Hell, the sinner ought to make every effort to die a happy death. Persevering prayer will obtain this grace for him. "Watch ye and pray," is Our Lord's admonition to all of us, "because ye know not the day nor the hour."

SUGGESTIONS FOR STUDY AND REVIEW

1. Who will be cast into Hell?
2. How do we know that the pains of the damned are eternal?
3. What are the sufferings of the damned?
4. Will the pains of the damned be equal?
5. Can we prove an eternal Hell from reason alone?
6. Mention *five parables* of Our Lord which end with the condemnation of the wicked to Hell.
7. In order to answer the objections so often brought against the Christian doctrine of Hell, remember (*a*) that God wishes all men to be saved and gives each one abundant grace to work out his salvation; (*b*) that all who are condemned to Hell are condemned through their own fault;

(*c*) that God cannot forgive a sin that is not repented of, and that after death there is no possibility of repenting. "Work whilst it is day; the night cometh wherein no man can work," says Our Lord; (*d*) that it is useless to speculate about the nature of the *pain of sense* in Hell, since it evidently exceeds our understanding; (*e*) that the Church did not invent the doctrine of eternal punishment, but that it is an article of the faith revealed by Christ Himself.

8. *Readings:*

    a) Luke 16,18-31.

    b) Matt. 25,1-13.

    c) *Imitation of Christ*, Bk. I, ch. 24.

CHAPTER XXIV

The Resurrection of the Dead and the General Judgment

"The hour cometh wherein all that are in the graves shall hear the voice of the Son of Man."—JOHN 5,28.

1. The Particular Judgment.—Our lot for all eternity is determined immediately after death. This decision on the part of God is called the Particular Judgment. "It is appointed unto man once to die and after that the judgment" (Heb. 9,27). Christ taught that the Rich Man and Lazarus went to their reward immediately after death (Luke 16,22). To the Penitent Thief He said: "This day thou shalt be with Me in Paradise" (Luke 23,43).

"The common opinion is that souls are judged at the time and in the place of death. God manifests to the soul by some interior illumination its state and its future lot, whereupon the soul, to borrow an illustration from St. Thomas, finds the place which belongs to it in Heaven, or Purgatory, or Hell, just as bodies find their place according to the law of gravity" (*Cath. Dict.*).

2. The End of the World.—When the end of the present world will be, we cannot tell. God has not revealed it. "Of that day and hour no one knoweth, no not the Angels of Heaven, but the Father alone" (Matt. 24,36). According to Scripture, certain events will precede the last day and herald its approach. These signs are:

a) The universal preaching of the Gospel (Matt. 24,14).
b) The conversion of great numbers of Jews (Rom. 11,25).
c) This conversion of the Jews will be accomplished by the Prophet *Elias* (Mal. 4,5-6).
d) Many Christians will apostatize, seduced by Antichrist (2 Thess. 2,2).
e) Many extraordinary disturbances of nature (Matt. 24,29).

3. Resurrection of the Body.—All men, the good as well as the wicked, shall rise again on the last day. This is a central dogma of Christianity. We find this doctrine taught in the later books of the Old Testament. In the Second Book of Machabees, the Martyr-Brothers are comforted amidst their torments with the hope

and belief that those very members which they are losing for
God's sake will be restored again to them by Him. The third eld-
est "quickly put forth his tongue, and courageously stretched out
his hands, and said with confidence: 'These I have from Heaven,
but for the laws of God I now despise them, because I hope to
receive them again from Him" (2 Mach. 7,10-11). Martha's words:
"I know that he [Lazarus] shall rise again in the resurrection at
the last day" (John 11,24), prove that belief in the resurrection
of the dead was prevalent among the Jewish people at the time of
Christ. The resurrection of the dead is the thirteenth article of the
Jewish Creed.

Our Lord teaches the doctrine of the resurrection in the most
unmistakable terms: "The hour cometh wherein all that are in the
graves shall hear the voice of the Son of God; and they that have
done good things shall come forth unto the resurrection of life;
but they that have done evil, unto the resurrection of judgment"
(John 5,28-29).

4. The Risen Body.—Every soul will be united to the same
body which it had in this life, in order that, as the body was its
partner in doing good or evil, it also may share its reward or
punishment. Even here on earth our bodies remain the same,
though the material substance of which they are composed is in
constant change.

According to the teaching of St. Paul, the risen body will have
four special qualities which our bodies do not at present possess:
(a) they will be *incapable of corruption* and of any suffering;
(b) they will *shine with glory*, that is, they will be without spot
or blemish; (c) they will have the *power* of transporting themselves in an instant from one place to another; (d) they will be
spiritualized, that is, capable of penetrating any corporeal substance. "The body," says St. Paul, "is sown [buried] in corruption, it shall rise in *incorruption*; it is sown in dishonor, it shall
rise in *glory*; it is sown in weakness, it shall rise in *power*; it is
sown a natural body, it shall rise a *spiritual body* (1 Cor. 15,42-44).

5. The General Judgment.—The resurrection of the dead
will be followed immediately by the General Judgment. "When
the Son of Man shall come in His majesty, and all the Angels
with Him, then shall He sit upon the seat of His majesty, and all
the nations shall be gathered together before Him, and He shall

separate them one from another, as the shepherd separateth the sheep from the goats" (Matt. 25,31-32).

In the Old Testament the Prophets speak of a great judgment which is to take place in the last days. From these prophecies the Jews derived their notion of a glorious and mighty Messias; and hence they rejected Our Lord, who came to them in poverty, humility and meekness. But He made it clear that these prophecies foretold His Second Coming in great power and majesty (Matt. 26,64).

The Apostles time and again preach the Second Coming of Christ in order to exhort their hearers to lead holy lives and to comfort them in their trials and sufferings. The doctrine of the General Judgment is also contained in all the ancient Creeds of the Church. "He sitteth at the right hand of God the Father Almighty," we read in the *Athanasian Creed*, "from whence He shall come to judge the living and the dead. At whose coming all men shall rise again with their bodies, and shall give an account of their works."

6. Purpose of the General Judgment.—The General Judgment is intended (*a*) to manifest before all intelligent creatures the *justice of God*; (*b*) to exhibit *Christ in His Majesty* before their eyes; (*c*) to *glorify the just* and to put the wicked to shame.

In order to attain this end God will enlighten the mind of each one concerning his own thoughts, words and deeds, and those of all others. The sins even of the just, it is believed, will be manifested, in order that the judgment may be complete, and that God's justice and mercy may shine forth.

7. Circumstances and Details of the Judgment.—The *time* of Our Lord's second coming has not been made known to us; but He continually warns us to be on the watch, so as not to be taken unawares. The place in which the Judgment will be held is here on earth. The neighborhood of Jerusalem, where Our Lord suffered and died and ascended into Heaven, would seem to be the most fitting place for His return and His final triumph. The *Judge* will be Our Lord Jesus Christ in His human nature as the Son of Man. "Neither doth the Father judge any man; but hath given all judgment to the Son . . . and He hath given Him power to do judgment because He is the Son of Man" (John 5,22,27). The *judged* will be all mankind, the good as well as the bad; those who are alive at the last day, as well as those who shall have died.

THE LAST JUDGMENT

"And then shall appear the sign of the Son of man in heaven: and then shall all tribes of the earth mourn: and they shall see the Son of man coming in the clouds of heaven with much power and majesty." (Matt. 24,30.)

The *account* will embrace all our works and sins, even our idle
words and most secret thoughts. Christ will judge all men according as they have believed in Him and have kept His commandments (John 3,16; Matt. 16,27).

8. The Sentence.—When "all nations shall be gathered together before Him, the Son of Man shall separate them one from
another, as the shepherd separateth the sheep from the goats; and
He shall set the sheep on His right hand, and the goats on His
left." Then He will pronounce sentence of reward or condemnation:

"Come,
Ye blessed of My Father,
Possess you the kingdom
Prepared for you from the
    foundation of the world."
	"Depart from Me,
	You cursed,
	Into everlasting fire
	Prepared for the devil
	    and his angels."

"And these shall go into everlasting punishment, but the just into
life everlasting" (Matt. 25,31ff.).

The confusion of the wicked and the triumph of the just is graphically
described in the *Book of Wisdom*:

"Then shall the just stand with great constancy
Against those that have afflicted them,
And taken away their labors.
These, seeing it, shall be troubled with terrible fear,
And shall be amazed at the suddenness of their unexpected salvation,
Saying within themselves, repenting,
And groaning for anguish of spirit:
These are they whom we had some time in derision,
And for a parable of reproach.
We fools esteemed their life madness,
And their end without honor.
Behold how they are numbered among the children of God,
And their lot is among the Saints.
Therefore we have erred . . . .

"But the just shall live for evermore,
And their reward is with the Lord,
And the care of them with the Most High.
Therefore shall they receive a kingdom of glory,
And a crown of beauty at the hand of the Lord."—*Wis.* 5,1-6,16-17.

9. A New Heaven and a New Earth.—The Day of Judgment
will close the present order of things. The time of probation will
have passed. Purgatory will cease to be; Heaven and Hell alone
will remain. This visible world of ours will be destroyed by fire.

"Come Ye Blessed of My Father"

175

The *great conflagration* will be followed by the *renovation* of the world: "The Day of the Lord shall come as a thief, in which the heavens shall pass away with great violence, and the elements shall be melted with heat, and the earth and the works which are in it shall be burnt up. . . . But we look for a *new earth* according to His promises, in which justice dwelleth" (2 Pet. 3,10-13).

St. John caught a glimpse of this *new Heaven* and *new Earth*: "And I saw a new heaven and a new earth, for the first heaven and the first earth was gone, and the sea is now no more. And I, John, saw the Holy City, the New Jerusalem, coming down out of heaven from God, prepared as a bride adorned for her husband. And I heard a great voice from the throne, saying: Behold the tabernacle of God with men! He will dwell with them, and they shall be His people, and God Himself with them shall be their God" (Apoc. 21,1-3).

SUGGESTIONS FOR STUDY AND REVIEW

1. What happens to the soul immediately after death?
2. How long will the body be in the earth?
3. How does the Church honor the bodies of the dead? Is *cremation* lawful?
4. How can the bodies, when reduced to dust, rise again?
5. What will follow immediately after the resurrection of the dead?
6. Why will there be a General Judgment besides the Particular?
7. What do the following texts tell us about the General Judgment: Matt. 24,36; Mark 13,22; Matt. 12,36; 1 Cor. 4,5; Apoc. 20,12; 2 Cor. 5,10?
8. Describe the circumstances of the Last Judgment: Time, place, the Judge, the judged, the account, the sentence.
9. What will happen after the General Judgment?
10. Read the grand Medieval Hymn *Dies Irae* by Thomas of Celano, whom St. Francis of Assisi himself received into the Franciscan Order in 1213. It has two parts: "Description of the Judgment" (vv.1-7) and "Prayers for mercy" (8-19).

Index

A COMPLETE SERIES

A COURSE IN RELIGION for Catholic High Schools and Academies. Fr. John Laux, M.A. 4-vol. set. PB. Impr. A set of 4 books, originally published in 1928, designed to give high school students a fantastic knowledge of their Faith. Also great for college and for adults to read on their own. Fr. Laux purposely wrote his books this way. One of the most gifted writers we have encountered: He is brief, clear, understandable and *interesting!* Moreover, he writes in a virtually undated and undatable manner, concentrating overall on the timeless truths of the Faith. Therefore, these books are *not* anachronisms! It is a *very rare* Catholic who would not learn a vast amount from any or all of these books!

1084 CHIEF TRUTHS OF THE FAITH—A Course in Religion, Book I. Fr. John Laux, M.A. 176 pp. PB. Impr. 54 Illus. Indexed. Suggestions for Study. The Sources of Faith; the Holy Scriptures; the Nature of God; the Mystery of the Holy Trinity; the Creation; the Redemption; Sanctification and Grace; and the Four Last Things. Best brief outline of our Faith we know. **8.00**

1085 MASS AND THE SACRAMENTS—A Course in Religion, Book II. Fr. John Laux, M.A. 199 pp. PB. Impr. 72 Illus. Indexed. Suggestions for Study. Covers the Seven Sacraments, the Holy Sacrifice of the Mass, sacramentals and indulgences, with an appendix containing the Ordinary of the Tridentine Mass in Latin and in English with rubrics and explanatory notes, plus illustrations of the traditional altar, priest's vestments and sacred vessels. **8.00**

1086 CATHOLIC MORALITY—A Course in Religion, Book III. Fr. John Laux, M.A. 164 pp. PB. Impr. 40 Illus. Indexed. Suggestions for study. A brief but complete book on traditional Catholic morality. Covers every basic aspect—the purpose of life, free will, the Natural Law, positive divine law, human positive laws, elements of a moral act, virtues, Christian perfection, Evangelical Counsels, nature of sin, kinds of sin, duties toward God, ourselves, our neighbor, the family, the state, the Church, etc. **8.00**

1087 CATHOLIC APOLOGETICS—A Course in Religion, Book IV. Fr. John Laux, M.A. 134 pp. PB. Impr. 38 Illus. Indexed. Suggestions for Study. This is one of the best apologetics books we have ever seen. Covers the nature of our knowledge and sources of our knowledge, justification for our belief, proofs for the existence of God, immortality of the soul, Revelation and evidence of Revelation, genuineness of the Gospels, claims of Jesus, reasonableness of our belief in the Church, nature of the Church, primacy of the Pope, his infallibility, etc. **8.00**

1083 INTRODUCTION TO THE BIBLE. Fr. John Laux, M.A. 326 pp. PB. Impr. 57 Illus. Indexed. Maps. Suggestions for Study. The nature, history, authorship and content of the Holy Bible, with selections from and commentaries on most of the various books. Covers Old and New Testaments. An excellent and unparalleled introduction to the Bible. Written originally as a textbook for students, but also intended by the author—as with all his books—for adult readership. **13.00**

0231 CHURCH HISTORY: A Complete History of the Catholic Church to the Present Day. Fr. John J. Laux, M.A. 659 pp. PB. 141 Illus. Index. Impr. Discussion questions for each chapter. If you ever wanted to know Church history and did not know where to start, this is the book. It was written by a master teacher for both students and adults. Anyone who becomes familiar with this book will have an *excellent* background in Church history. We know no other book that gives such a wealth of information in such an absorbing manner. **20.00**

At your bookdealer or direct from the Publisher.

Prices guaranteed through 12/31/91.

If you have enjoyed this book, consider making your next selection from among the following . . .

Prices guaranteed through December 31, 1992.

Raised from the Dead. Fr. Hebert 13.50
Love and Service of God, Infinite Love. Mother Louise Margaret. 10.00
Life and Work of Mother Louise Margaret. Fr. O'Connell 10.00
Autobiography of St. Margaret Mary 4.00
Thoughts and Sayings of St. Margaret Mary 3.00
The Voice of the Saints. Comp. by Francis Johnston 5.00
The 12 Steps to Holiness and Salvation. St. Alphonsus 6.00
The Rosary and the Crisis of Faith. Cirrincione & Nelson 1.25
Sin and Its Consequences. Cardinal Manning 5.00
Fourfold Sovereignty of God. Cardinal Manning 5.00
Catholic Apologetics Today. Fr. Most 8.00
Dialogue of St. Catherine of Siena. Transl. Algar Thorold 9.00
Catholic Answer to Jehovah's Witnesses. D'Angelo 8.00
Twelve Promises of the Sacred Heart. (100 cards) 5.00
St. Aloysius Gonzaga. Fr. Meschler 10.00
The Love of Mary. D. Roberto 7.00
Begone Satan. Fr. Vogl 2.00
The Prophets and Our Times. Fr. R. G. Culleton 10.00
St. Therese, The Little Flower. John Beevers 4.50
St. Joseph of Copertino. Fr. Angelo Pastrovicchi 4.50
Mary, The Second Eve. Cardinal Newman 2.50
Devotion to Infant Jesus of Prague. Booklet 75
The Faith of Our Fathers. Cardinal Gibbons 13.00
The Wonder of Guadalupe. Francis Johnston 6.00
Apologetics. Msgr. Paul Glenn 9.00
Baltimore Catechism No. 1 . . . . 3.00
Baltimore Catechism No. 2 . . . . 4.00
Baltimore Catechism No. 3 . . . . 7.00
An Explanation of the Baltimore Catechism. Fr. Kinkead 13.00
Bethlehem. Fr. Faber 13.50
Bible History. Schuster 10.00
Blessed Eucharist. Fr. Mueller 13.00
Catholic Catechism. Fr. Faerber 5.00
The Devil. Fr. Delaporte 5.00
Dogmatic Theology for the Laity. Fr. Premm 15.00
Evidence of Satan in the Modern World. Cristiani 8.50
Fifteen Promises of Mary. (100 cards) 5.00
Life of Anne Catherine Emmerich. 2 vols. Schmoger 37.50
Life of the Blessed Virgin Mary. Emmerich 13.50
Manual of Practical Devotion to St. Joseph. Patrignani 12.50
Prayer to St. Michael. (100 leaflets) 5.00
Prayerbook of Favorite Litanies. Fr. Hebert 8.50
Preparation for Death. (Abridged). St. Alphonsus 7.00
Purgatory Explained. Schouppe 12.50
Purgatory Explained. (pocket, unabr.). Schouppe 5.00
Fundamentals of Catholic Dogma. Ludwig Ott 16.50
Spiritual Conferences. Tauler 10.00
Trustful Surrender to Divine Providence. Bl. Claude 4.00
Wife, Mother and Mystic. Bessieres 7.00
The Agony of Jesus. Padre Pio 1.00

Prices guaranteed through December 31, 1992.

Prices guaranteed through December 31, 1992.

At your bookdealer or direct from the publisher.

Prices guaranteed through December 31, 1992.